THE GOSPEL FOR THE CHURCH
Rediscovering the Power of the Cross

setting
CAPTIVES free

THE GOSPEL FOR
THE CHURCH

— Rediscovering the Power of the Cross —

ERICK HURT

SETTING CAPTIVES FREE
PUBLISHING

Cover Design: Melissa K. Thomas

Setting Captives Free Publishing
Jackson, WY

ISBN: 978-1-7337609-7-3
LCCN: 2020916835

Table of Contents

Acknowledgments

*I*f there has been a man who has shown and shared the love of Christ so affectionately, laboring night and day for the sake of Christ, it would be my brother, friend, and partner in ministry, Mike Cleveland. Everyone he meets becomes near and dear to him as he gives his life away to proclaim tirelessly the message of the cross. In fact, I can image Mike and Jody, his wonderful wife, writing something like this:

> *"So, being affectionately desirous of you, we were ready to share with you not only the gospel of God but also our own selves, because you had become very dear to us. 9 For you remember, brothers, our labor and toil: we worked night and day, that we might not be a burden to any of you, while we proclaimed to you the gospel of God." 1 Thessalonians 2:8-9*

Together, Mike and Jody Cleveland have shown me more accurately the gospel of Jesus Christ (Acts 18:26) as they have shared not only the gospel with me but their very own lives. They have labored to lighten the load of many and like Jesus have laid down their lives for their friends (John 15:13).

Mike and Jody, thank you for your many hours of prayer, editing, guidance, instruction, and laboring with me to make this book possible. Without your help and partnership in the gospel (the death and resurrection of Jesus Christ), this writing would not exist.

Foreword by Mike Cleveland,
Founder of Setting Captives Free

*L*oyalty programs are quite popular these days. To join, all you need to do is offer up your name and phone number. One step, and now you are a loyal member of the community and entitled to all the benefits of it.

Many churches have adopted this approach as well. Just "pray the sinner's prayer", raise your hand in response to a message, walk an aisle indicating your decision to follow Christ, or fill out a connection card, and you will be added to the community as a disciple of Jesus Christ.

But is this what becoming a disciple of Jesus Christ is all about?

Jesus Christ, after His death and resurrection, was given all authority in heaven and on earth, and as the Head of the Church He has instructed us to "Therefore, go and make disciples of all nations…" (Matthew 28:19). All believers are to be engaged in making disciples, and we minister in Jesus' name and with Jesus' authority when engaged in this work of making disciples.

But what is a true disciple of Jesus Christ? And how do we make disciples? What message do we use in making disciples, and what is the evidence that someone is a disciple of Jesus Christ?

This course is written to anyone who wants to take the instruction of Jesus Christ to heart, to *"go and make disciples of all nations."* It is written for church leaders, church members, and non-churchgoers; any and all who want to know what it means to be a disciple of Jesus Christ, and how to make a disciple of Jesus Christ.

Come and learn from God's Word, as taught by Setting Captives Free Board Member Erick Hurt, on what true disciple making is. Let's pray that the church, worldwide, catches the passion that Jesus had as He went to the cross, suffered and died, then rose again to make disciples!

Introduction

"Behold, I stand at the door [of the church] and continually knock. If anyone hears My voice and opens the door, I will come in and eat with him (restore him), and he with Me." Revelation 3:20 AMP

Today, Jesus is standing at the door of many churches knocking. He desires to come in and eat with believers—to be intimate and close to us—the church. But why is the door not opened to Him? How is it that the rightful owner who purchased the church with His blood is standing outside? Why is Jesus continually knocking?

A "lukewarm" church (Revelation 3:16) is a church that has abandoned the message of the cross. The cross is no longer the central part of sermons and teachings, which has left Jesus on the outside with the door closed, knocking and waiting.

The cross is the message of power (Romans 1:16; 1 Corinthians 1:18), and if it's lost its place of "first importance" (1 Corinthians 15:3) in the church, the very foundation of the church is compromised. If we invite others to fill its place, "good speakers" and "good programs," we close the church's door to the One who purchased her with His precious blood.

> *"He who overcomes [the world through believing that Jesus is the Son of God], I will grant to him [the privilege] to sit beside Me on My throne, as I also overcame and sat down beside My Father on His throne."*

In Revelation 3:21, the promise to the overcoming church is connected to the power of the gospel. Jesus died on the cross and overcame death through resurrection power, then ascended to the Father, was accepted and seated on His throne. Our overcoming of the world, the flesh, and the devil is tied to the ongoing hearing of *this* message.

Oh, friend, may the church worldwide return wholeheartedly to the message of the cross that we might see many people die to sin and rise with Jesus to new life. The church opens the door to Jesus when we commit to the message He gave us, that of His suffering and dying for our sin and rising from the dead. This course is an invitation to open the door to Jesus, through returning to the message of the cross, that we might experience wonderful and intimate fellowship with Jesus.

The Chief Goal of the Church

*L*et's begin by examining the church's chief responsibility known as "The Great Commission", given by Jesus prior to His ascension into heaven.

> *"And Jesus came and said to them, "All authority in heaven and on earth has been given to me. ¹⁹ Go therefore and make disciples of all nations, baptizing them in the name of the Father and of the Son and of the Holy Spirit, ²⁰ teaching them to observe all that I have commanded you. And behold, I am with you always, to the end of the age." Matthew 28:18-20*

Question 1: According to Matthew 28:18-20 what is the primary function of all believers in Jesus Christ, the church?
- ☐ To live in community with one another.
- ☐ To make disciples of all nations.
- ☐ To care for the poor and needy.

Yes, the main purpose of the church is to go and make disciples of all nations, to baptize and teach them to observe all that Jesus commanded. So we put programs together and find those in our church willing to lend a helping hand. We use any means we can find to assist in this chief mission of making disciples of all nations.

But what makes one a disciple of Jesus Christ? Is it making a decision, walking an aisle, or promising to do your best to follow Jesus? Is it saying the words, "I believe in Jesus Christ" and therefore I'm now a disciple of Jesus ready to make other disciples of Jesus? How can we make disciples and know that we're making them as Jesus commanded?

In Jesus' opening statement of "The Great Commission," He declared, "*All authority in heaven and on earth has been given to me*" (Matthew 28:18).

It's important to understand that the foundation upon which Jesus received all authority in heaven and on earth is His work on the cross and His resurrection from the dead. In other words, because Jesus died and rose again, He has been given all authority, "in heaven and on" earth".

Notice the text prior to Jesus making this monumental statement about "All authority" being given to Him in heaven and on earth, and we will see that Jesus' authority flows out of the gospel:

> "*Now after the Sabbath, toward the dawn of the first day of the week, Mary Magdalene and the other Mary went to see the tomb. ² And behold, there was a great earthquake, for an angel of the Lord descended from heaven and came and rolled back the stone and sat on it. ³ His appearance was like lightning, and his clothing white as snow. ⁴ And for fear of him the guards trembled and became like dead men. ⁵ But the angel said to the women, "Do not be afraid, for I know that you seek Jesus who was crucified. ⁶ He is not here, for he has risen, as he said. Come, see the place where he lay." Matthew 28:1-6*

Question 2: According to Matthew 28:1-6 what event took place before Jesus had declared that, "All authority" has been given to Him?
- ☐ Jesus was crucified, was buried in a tomb, and has risen
- ☐ Jesus was baptized and led into the wilderness to be tempted.
- ☐ Jesus changed water into wine.

Jesus Christ has been given all authority, "in heaven", and "on earth" because He died on the cross for our sins and rose victorious on the third day. Yes, Jesus was crucified, buried in a tomb, and raised from the dead, and this is the event Jesus was referring to, the good news of the gospel. The gospel then becomes the foundation upon which Jesus' authority rests.

And this gospel is the message that makes disciples. The gospel is the message that defines a disciple as one who has died with Christ and been raised up to a new life in Jesus (2 Corinthians 5:17). The gospel is the one message that *cuts the hearts* of its hearers (Acts 2:37). Any other message other than the gospel message is void of the power of God because the gospel is the *"power of God."*

> *"For I am not ashamed of the gospel, for it is the power of God for salvation to everyone who believes, to the Jew first and also to the Greek." Romans 1:16*

Not only is it the power for salvation but also power for those being saved.

> *"For the word of the cross is folly to those who are perishing, but to us who are being saved it is the power of God." 1 Corinthians 1:18*

And this is why we read in 1 Corinthians 15:3-4 that the gospel is of *"first importance."*

> *"For I delivered to you as of first importance what I also received: that Christ died for our sins in accordance with the Scriptures, 4 that he was buried, that he was raised on the third day in accordance with the Scriptures," 1 Corinthians 15:3-4*

There is nothing more powerful and nothing of equal value. It is the gospel that is the heart of the message of the church. It is the gospel that transforms the heart and mind making one a new creation. It is the gospel where we find the forgiveness of sins. And it is through believing the gospel that we die with Christ and are raised to new life. This is why it is always of first importance.

Question 3: It's critical that we define the gospel, for often it happens that a person thinks they are holding to or preaching the gospel when in truth they haven't seen it clearly defined in Scripture. According to 1 Corinthians 15:3-4, what is the gospel?

_____

_____

_____

_____

If you said: *"that Christ died for our sins in accordance with the Scriptures, that he was buried, that he was raised on the third day in accordance with the Scriptures,"* you're right! Our ministry here at Setting Captives Free is a *"gospel only"* ministry in which we share the gospel with students and help them apply it to their lives to find freedom from habitual sins.

The "good news" of the gospel is always one message with two parts:
1. Jesus died for our sins according to the Scriptures.
2. Jesus was raised on the third day according to the Scriptures.

Question 4: While making disciples what is the "one message" Jesus wants us to share?
- ☐ The gospel or good news of Jesus Christ
- ☐ The gospel or good news of the Cross
- ☐ The gospel, that Jesus died for our sins, was buried and rose on the third day

Problems and errors in life always come when we turn away from this message, and begin to "ad-lib" with our own message. We notice this clearly in the Book of Galatians:

> *"I am astonished that you are so quickly deserting him who called you in the grace of Christ and are turning to a different gospel—*
> *⁷not that there is another one, but there are some who trouble*

you and want to distort the gospel of Christ. [8] *But even if we or an angel from heaven should preach to you a gospel contrary to the one we preached to you, let him be accursed.* [9] *As we have said before, so now I say again: If anyone is preaching to you a gospel contrary to the one you received, let him be accursed."*
Galatians 1:6-9

Question 5: According to Galatians 1:6, what was the error of the Galatians? Fill in the Blank: "I am astonished that you are so quickly deserting _____ _____ _____ _____ in the grace of Christ and are turning to a _____ _____."

There may be many different gospels even in the church today, just as there was when this letter was written to the Galatians. A few examples might be the books, programs, or counseling methods accepted today where the goal for those receiving counsel is "recovery" rather than to "die with Christ." To "get better" rather than to rise from the dead as a "new creation" which brings freedom from sins slavery and power.

However, this is not "counseling from the cross" but a different gospel and therefore not helpful. It's missing "the power of God" (Romans 1:16) in Jesus' death and resurrection. It is the message of the cross that "cuts our hearts" doing the work for us and in us.

When we receive the Spirit (hearing the message of the cross by faith) He continues to work His transforming power in us for the rest of our lives. The cross and the Spirit do what no man could possibly do by transforming our lives "on the inside," in our hearts, making us into the image of Christ.

Question 6: Why is it important that we do not preach a "different gospel - not that there is another one"? Please share your thoughts.

_____

_____

_____

_____

This is why our desire here at Setting Captives Free is to be a gospel only ministry. We do not want to turn from the One who purchased us and forgave our sin with His blood while on the cross for us. We do not want our message to change into a different gospel which has no power to change the human heart.

We want to lift up the one message that has the power to change the heart, the gospel, which means "good news." Remember the good news is always one message with two parts; 1) that Jesus died for our sins according to the Scriptures, and was buried, and 2) Jesus was raised on the third day according to the Scriptures and was seen by many.

> *"I am astonished that you are so quickly deserting him who called you in the grace of Christ and are turning to a different gospel— ⁷not that there is another one, but there are some who trouble you and want to distort the gospel of Christ." Galatians 1:6-7*

Question 7: According to Galatians 1:7 what is the purpose of another gospel?
- ☐ To triumph and harmonize all religions with the gospel of Christ.
- ☐ To cause trouble and distort the gospel of Christ
- ☐ To bring clarity and open up the new age gospel of Christ

Yes, the purpose of "another gospel" is to trouble others and distort the gospel of Christ. Notice Acts 20:29-31:

"I know that after my departure fierce wolves will come in among you, not sparing the flock; [30] *and from among your own selves will arise men speaking twisted things, to draw away the disciples after them.* [31] *Therefore be alert, remembering that for three years I did not cease night or day to admonish every one with tears." Acts 20:29-31*

Question 8: How does Acts 20:29-31 apply to our study today? And why was Paul warning them with tears?
- ☐ Friendly wolves are coming and the church should welcome them just as they should welcome anyone else
- ☐ Fierce wolves are coming but they will spare the flock so we do not need to worry but just trust and obey
- ☐ Fierce wolves are coming and will not spare the flock, speaking twisted things to draw disciples after themselves

Yes, fierce wolves are coming in and will not spare the flock. They will come in using a different "gospel" which are "twisted things" to draw away disciples after themselves. Therefore we are to be alert and on our guard because once the wolves leave with the sheep it will be too late for us to share the gospel with them. So fierce wolves will not be coming in announcing that they're about to draw away disciples after themselves, but through words contrary to the true gospel will draw disciples after them using twisted things.

These are not like the wolves we may hear through the night as they surround their prey to go in and devour them. No, if that was the case then the world would be able to notice them too. But these wolves come "in sheep's clothing". So the wolves will look like sheep, smell like sheep, and act like sheep so that their only distinction will be their false gospel or twisted things.

"Beware of false prophets, who come to you in sheep's clothing but inwardly are ravenous wolves." Matthew 7:15

Friend, we must be very careful to preach and teach the gospel of Jesus Christ (1 Corinthians 15:3-4) which is the only way to "protect the flock."

Notice from Acts 20:28-31 that the "flock" is protected by the "blood" Jesus shed on the cross.

There is an amazing illustration of the blood of Jesus protecting the church. In the Middle East, there is a particular kind of worm called a Tolah (the word means "crimson"), and it has a certain characteristic: when the Tolah is pregnant and about to give birth it climbs up in a tree and uses a twig of the tree to pierce its own heart so that the resultant blood flow will produce a cocoon-like shelter for its young. The tolah worm literally sheds its own blood, gives its own life to protect its children. In Psalm 22 (the "Psalm of the Cross"), this is the very word Jesus used, when speaking through David He said, "But I am like a worm (tolah) and not a man" (Psalm 22:6).

The blood of Jesus protects the church (and therefore the sheep) from a distorted gospel thereby sparing the flock. The gospel of Jesus Christ protects the church from those who would seek to bring in destructive teachings.

> *"Pay careful attention to yourselves and to all the flock, in which the Holy Spirit has made you overseers, to care for the church of God, which he obtained with his own blood." Acts 20:28*

> *"But even if we or an angel from heaven should preach to you a gospel contrary to the one we preached to you, let him be accursed. 9 As we have said before, so now I say again: If anyone is preaching to you a gospel contrary to the one you received, let him be accursed." Galatians 1:8-9*

> *"But false prophets also arose among the people, just as there will be false teachers among you, who will secretly bring in destructive heresies, even denying the Master who bought them, bringing upon themselves swift destruction." 2 Peter 2:1*

Question 9: How do Jesus' death and resurrection protect the church from "destructive heresies," according to the passages and illustration above?

Yes, "destructive heresies" come from those who deny the Master who bought them. They deny both the Master and the purchase He made at the cross. They deny the blood He shed to purchase His people, the cross He died on to make us righteous, the payment He made at the cost of His life.

The church is protected when it is focused on this purchase price made at the cross when it is focused on "the Master who bought them." And more disciples are made, that is, those who put faith in the message of the cross and who enter into the death and resurrection of Jesus Christ themselves.

And isn't this the goal of the church? To make disciples of all nations? In order to do so, the church must focus like a laser on the gospel of Jesus Christ!

Question 10: Why is it important for the church to clearly define and clearly preach the gospel of Jesus Christ?

The Gospel—One Message With Two Parts:
The Death

Welcome back to the course, The Gospel for the Church. We are so thankful to have you back studying with us.

Today, we're going to be focusing our attention on one of the two parts of the gospel. As we stated in lesson 1, the gospel is really "one message" with two parts: 1) Jesus died for our sins according to the Scriptures. 2) Jesus was raised on the third day according to the Scriptures (1 Corinthians 15:3-4). So, today we'll focus our attention on the cross, or the first part of the gospel.

The "good news" of **the gospel** is **one message** with two parts:

1. **The death**
2. The resurrection

Let's notice the central importance of the death of Jesus, as well as the results of it, as described in Ephesians 1:

> *"...even as he chose us in him before the foundation of the world, that we should be holy and blameless before him. In love* [5] *he predestined us for adoption to himself as sons through Jesus Christ, according to the purpose of his will,* [6] *to the praise of his glorious grace, with which he has blessed us in the Beloved.* [7] *In him, we have redemption through his blood, the forgiveness of our trespasses, according to the riches of his grace." Ephesians 1:4-7*

Question 1: According to Ephesians 1:4, when did God plan on sending His Son to the cross, and what was the purpose?
- ☐ Before Adam and Eve were born, to restore the garden.
- ☐ Before He made the stars in the heavens, to renew creation.
- ☐ Before the foundation of the world; that we should be holy and blameless before Him.

Question 2: Who were all believers "adopted to," and what was the price paid according to Ephesians 1:4-7? "In love He predestined us for adoption ____ _____ as sons through Jesus Christ...in Him we have _____ _____ _____ _____."

Yes, God "chose us" in Him before the foundation of the world that we should be "holy and blameless before him" and *"in love"* He adopted us (you were legally made His child) to Himself to become children "through Jesus Christ." That is, through His death on the cross, He purchased our adoption with blood. This was the purpose of His will and *"to the praise of his glorious grace."*

Now think about this just for a moment with me. At the cross Jesus would become as if he were unholy, and He was blamed for your sin, so you would become holy and blameless. At the cross Jesus, "The Son," was rejected by His Father so you could be accepted by being adopted *"as sons"* through Jesus Christ to the Father. Jesus, who knew no sin, became sin for you to purchase your adoption with His life so you could become part of the family of God.

"In him, we have redemption through his blood, the forgiveness of our trespasses, according to the riches of his grace," Ephesians 1:7

Question 3: According to Ephesians 1:7, what is the height, or pinnacle of God's rich grace, and what have we received as a result of it?

_____

_____

_____

_____

Friend, isn't' it amazing that God would "buy us back" or "purchase" us through the blood of Jesus while on the cross? The cross is the pinnacle of God's rich grace, the place He purchased the forgiveness of our trespasses and sins. It's the place we became holy and blameless and the place Jesus became sin for us, *"For our sake he made him to be sin who knew no sin"* (2 Corinthians 5:21).

Notice again the importance of the cross, and the accomplishments of it:

> *"For God has done what the law, weakened by the flesh, could not do. By sending his own Son in the likeness of sinful flesh and for sin, he condemned sin in the flesh" Romans 8:3*

Do you see that Jesus was condemned on the cross, in His flesh, and in your place? This is why there isn't any condemnation for those who are in Christ Jesus (Romans 8:1). Because Jesus was crushed on the cross you are made whole. Because Jesus was judged on the cross you are set free. Because Jesus became a curse on the cross you receive God's blessing (Galatians 3:13; Deuteronomy 21:23). *"For God did not send his Son into the world to condemn the world, but in order that the world might be saved through him"* (John 3:17). Saved "through" the doorway of the cross where Jesus was condemned, and we were set free!

Question 4: According to Romans 8:3, what did God do because the law was weakened by the flesh?
- ☐ He sent his own Son in the likeness of sinful flesh and for sin, he condemned sin in the flesh.
- ☐ He re-wrote His thoughts in the New Testament.
- ☐ He overlooks sin because He's a good, good Father.

Now notice from Ephesians 2:1-3 that God's wrath was coming for us! It states that by nature we were, *"children of wrath,"* the *"objects of God's wrath."* God was coming to put us to death to judge our sin! But the wrath of God was poured out on the cross and Jesus became our shield! Jesus bore our sin! Jesus took our place! God, *"condemned sin the flesh,"* in the flesh of His only Son! Friend, we have escaped, not because we ran and hid like Adam, but because Jesus, *"who for the joy that was set before him endured the cross" (Hebrews 12:2).*

> *"And you were dead in the trespasses and sins [2] in which you once walked, following the course of this world, following the prince of the power of the air, the spirit that is now at work in the sons of disobedience—* [3]*among whom we all once lived in the passions of our flesh, carrying out the desires of the body and the mind, and* **were by nature children of wrath**, *like the rest of mankind."*
> *Ephesians 2:1-3*

This passage tells us that we were "dead" in the trespasses and sins in which we "once walked." We were the original "walking dead" as we followed the course of this world and the devil who is the prince of the power of the air. So this makes sense that in our sinful nature we were by nature "children of wrath," and "walking dead" by living in our sinful passions.

> **Question 5:** We make disciples by preaching the message of the cross and seeing people who believe that message become crucified with Christ and risen from the dead.
> ☐ True
> ☐ False

Yes, this is true discipleship, when people grasp the message of the cross to the extent that they enter into the power of it themselves, where they are "crucified with Christ"(Galatians 2:20) and "risen with Christ" (Colossians 3:1).

The cross not only highlights Jesus' death for our sins, being condemned so we could be set free, taking on the sin of the entire world; it also shows Him taking on the sin debt that we could not pay. He *"canceled the charge of our legal indebtedness, which stood against us and condemned us; he has taken it away, nailing it to the cross"* (Colossians 2:14 NIV). When Jesus was nailed to the cross our debt was canceled. This is why the Scripture says, *"He became sin who knew no sin"* so that He could cancel the debt we owed but could not pay. *"This is the LORD's doing; it is marvelous in our eyes"* (Psalm 118:23).

> **Question 6:** Just how did Jesus cancel the charge of our legal indebtedness?
> ☐ He told His Father to cancel the debt because of His love for us.
> ☐ He asked His Father to cancel the debt because we are good people.
> ☐ He has taken it away, nailing it to the cross.

In other words, Jesus' flesh became our sin and was judged, condemned, and nailed to the cross as full payment of our sin debt.

But the cross is not merely the payment of our sin debt, glorious as that is, it is also where you and I die and live:

> *"I have been crucified with Christ. It is no longer I who live, but Christ who lives in me. And the life I now live in the flesh I live by faith in the Son of God, who loved me and gave himself for me." Galatians 2:20*

So, at the cross, we "have been crucified" with Christ and no longer live. In other words, we have joined Jesus in His death on the cross "by faith." We can clearly see that this is not a physical death because when we die physically we will not need faith to do it. But when we see Jesus hanging on the cross for us, *as us,* and because of our sin, it changes our heart and "by faith" we join Him in His death on the cross.

Did you notice how Galatians 2:20 begins and ends with the cross? I have been "crucified with Christ" is followed by "who loved me and gave Himself for me." Both of these statements regarding "the cross" are connected "by faith."

Now let's look at an example from the Old Testament:

"And the people spoke against God and against Moses, "Why have you brought us up out of Egypt to die in the wilderness? For there is no food and no water, and we loathe this worthless food." ⁶Then the Lord sent fiery serpents among the people, and they bit the people so that many people of Israel died. ⁷And the people came to Moses and said, "We have sinned, for we have spoken against the Lord and against you. Pray to the Lord, that he take away the serpents from us." So Moses prayed for the people." Numbers 21:5-7

Question 7: According to Numbers 21:5-6, what was the condition of the people?

_____

_____

_____

_____

Yes, they grumbled against the Lord and Moses and did not remember the Lord had freed them from their many years of bitter labor trapped in slavery. And they loathed the Manna which came to them without labor, efforts of their own but free food from heaven.

They recognized their sin, many were dying, and the people asked Moses to pray for them. So Moses prayed to the Lord and the Lord gave Moses a strange solution.

"And the Lord said to Moses, "Make a fiery serpent and set it on a pole, and everyone who is bitten, when he sees it, shall live." ⁹So Moses made a bronze serpent and set it on a pole. And if a serpent bit anyone, he would look at the bronze serpent and live." Numbers 21:8-9

Now we see that if anyone was bitten, instead of dying, all they had to do was "look at the bronze serpent" and live. They needed to look and believe. Or look "by faith" at the bronze serpent and live. This is exactly what Jesus said of Himself, that when we "look" and "believe" we who have been bitten by the snakebite of sin, would live!

> *"And as Moses lifted up the serpent in the wilderness, so must the Son of Man be lifted up,* [15] *that whoever believes in him may have eternal life.* [16]*For God so loved the world, that he gave his only Son, that whoever believes in him should not perish but have eternal life." John 3:14-16*

Jesus here is saying that as Moses "lifted up the serpent" in the wilderness, He, Jesus, would likewise be "lifted up" on the cross. And just like the cure was to look at the bronze serpent (which represented Jesus lifted up on the cross) and be healed from the "fiery serpents," we look to Jesus hanging there on the pole canceling our debt, forgiving our sins, and combined with faith, we are healed by His wounds from the poison of sin and death or the snakebite of sin and death.

Question 8: According to John 3:14-6, healing from the "fiery serpents," lifting up the serpent on a pole and "looking at it" for healing is related to Jesus being lifted up on a cross. What should we encourage people to do to be saved?
- ☐ Have them accept Jesus as their personal Savior.
- ☐ Have them repeat the sinner's prayer following your lead.
- ☐ Set the cross before them and Invite them to look to the cross with "eyes of faith", to believe the message of the cross, and thereby be healed from the snakebite of sin.

In this lesson, we focused on the first part of the gospel, the death of Jesus Christ, and its effects and benefits in the life of all who believe it. This is our message! It is the message that the church has been given to proclaim and to live!

It is my hope that you are seeing the power of this message to crucify and raise all who put faith in it, thereby making them disciples of Jesus Christ.

In our next lesson, we will continue on and discuss the importance of the gospel for the church.

Resting In Christ

*W*elcome back to the course!

Today we'll look at the burial of Jesus Christ. It is critical that we preach and teach with the one message Jesus told us to *"Go and make disciples of all nations"* with; the message that keeps us grounded and free from becoming distorted with *"another gospel."* This is the one message that keeps our lives stable, at peace, filled with joy, and changes our very nature (our hearts) on the inside. The message of the cross has the power to make us new creations!

To begin today's study, notice how God made the life and experiences of the Old Testament prophet, Jonah, to be a signpost pointing forward to the gospel of Jesus Christ:

> *"For just as Jonah was three days and three nights in the belly of the great fish, so will the Son of Man be three days and three nights in the heart of the earth." Matthew 12:40*

After Jesus' suffering on the cross for our sins He would "rest" from His work for *"three days and three nights"* in the heart of the earth. If the cross was where the battle was won, *"...having disarmed the powers and authorities, he made a public spectacle of them, triumphing over them by the cross"* (Colossians 2:15), then the grave is where Jesus found rest from His work.

> *"Therefore, while the promise of entering his rest still stands, let us fear lest any of you should seem to have failed to reach it. ² For good news came to us just as to them, but the message they heard did not benefit them, because they were not united by faith with those who listened." Hebrews 4:1-2*

Question 1: Hebrews 4 states that "good news" came but the message they heard "did not benefit them" and kept them from entering "his rest." Just what was it that kept them from entering this rest?

☐ They were great listeners who didn't need to have faith.

☐ They were not united "by faith" with those who listened.

☐ They were not united because they didn't hear the good news.

You may remember in lesson 1 *"being crucified with Christ"* was to be joined "by faith" (see Galatians 2:20). Here we see the same promise of *"resting"* one can enter into when united by faith. It isn't "what we do" but how we find rest in what Jesus did on the cross. And this rest is connected with the work Jesus finished on the cross for the church. We are united in Jesus' death and burial by believing the *"good news,"* as faith comes by *"hearing"* and hearing the Word (gospel) of Christ.

> *"But they have not all obeyed the gospel. For Isaiah says, "Lord, who has believed what he has heard from us?" [17]So faith comes from hearing, and hearing through the word of Christ" Romans 10:16-17*

So we share the word of Christ, that Jesus died for you, that he bled for you, that He was torn for you, that He breathed His last breath for you. Then He was buried in a tomb and took your sins and mine to the grave where Jesus *"rested from His work"* as God rested from His.

> *"For he has somewhere spoken of the seventh day in this way: "And God rested on the seventh day from all his works." [5]And again in this passage, he said, "They shall not enter my rest." [6]Since, therefore, it remains for some to enter it, and those who formerly received the good news failed to enter because of disobedience, [7]again he appoints a certain day, "Today," saying through David so long afterward, in the words already quoted, "Today, if you hear his voice, do not harden your hearts." Hebrews 4:4-7*

Friend, when we minister to others, we must deliver the message of the gospel which keeps our focus on Jesus' finished work. We aren't sharing programs or the "works" of man, but we are teaching, preaching and testifying, that the church might hear by faith, believe the message over and over, and enter into God's rest.

> *"For if Joshua had given them rest, God would not have spoken of another day later on. ⁹So then, there remains a Sabbath rest for the people of God, ¹⁰for whoever has entered God's rest has also rested from his works as God did from his." Hebrews 4:8-10*

Do you see it? There remains a "Sabbath rest" for who? "The people of God." That is, you and I who by faith have heard the message and believe that Jesus died to set captives free and give us rest through His work on the cross!

This is the message that not only needs to be preached and taught but needs to be heard to bring life and freedom! It is by believing the gospel message by faith that we join in Jesus' death on the cross, are buried in the grave, and we find rest with Him. In other words, by believing the message of the cross, we have obeyed the Sabbath Day and the command to "rest" on it. Our old man rests in the grave with Jesus just as He rested on the Sabbath. And what are we resting from? Our own works of righteousness, programs, step groups, and philosophies.

> *"...he saved us, not because of works done by us in righteousness, but according to his own mercy, by the washing of regeneration and renewal of the Holy Spirit" Titus 3:5*

Question 2: Since Jesus rested on the Sabbath Day in the grave, keeping it holy, (Exodus 20:8), fulfilling the law perfectly, we enter into Jesus' rest from our own labor and efforts trying to find freedom from sin.
☐ True
☐ False

Jesus Christ fulfilled the law perfectly and by faith in Him we rest from our own efforts and programs (Romans 10:4), our own understanding, and we submit to the mercy and washing and renewal we receive at the cross. We know that we are not saved by obeying the law because one who attempts to obey the law must obey it perfectly and continuously (Galatians 3:10), and we see that following the law is opposed to living "by faith" in the finished work Jesus has done on the cross.

As we preach or teach the good news to others, we invite them to look at the work Jesus has done on the cross and how He is the end of the law for righteousness (Romans 10:4). By seeing Jesus dying for us, fulfilling the law perfectly, "by faith" we are deemed to have fulfilled the law perfectly in Christ (Romans 8:4).

> **Question 3:** According to Romans 8:4 and Romans 10:4, what do we see by faith when we look at the cross?
> - ☐ We see Jesus losing the battle to Satan, being crucified in weakness, and being buried forever.
> - ☐ We see that Jesus' perfect life and substitutionary death has made us righteous and that God now sees us as having perfectly fulfilled His law.
> - ☐ We see Jesus' love and grace, His mercy toward us, and forgiveness of our sins.

> *"Now it is evident that no one is justified before God by the law, for "The righteous shall live by faith." [12]But the law is not of faith, rather "The one who does them shall live by them." [13]Christ redeemed us from the curse of the law by becoming a curse for us—for it is written, "Cursed is everyone who is hanged on a tree"* Galatians 3:11-13

Notice what the Scriptures teach regarding faith. Faith in the message of the cross is…

Faith to join Christ in crucifixion

"I have been crucified with Christ. It is no longer I who live, but Christ who lives in me. And the life I now live in the flesh I live by faith in the Son of God, who loved me and gave himself for me." Galatians 2:20

Faith to join Christ in rest

"Therefore, while the promise of entering his rest still stands, let us fear lest any of you should seem to have failed to reach it. ²For good news came to us just as to them, but the message they heard did not benefit them, because they were not united by faith with those who listened." Hebrews 4:1-2

"For by grace you have been saved through faith. And this is not your own doing; it is the gift of God, ⁹not a result of works, so that no one may boast." Ephesians 2:8-9

"But far be it from me to boast except in the cross of our Lord Jesus Christ, by which the world has been crucified to me, and I to the world." Galatians 6:14

"We were buried therefore with him by baptism into death, in order that, just as Christ was raised from the dead by the glory of the Father, we too might walk in newness of life." Romans 6:4

Question 4: What do the above passages teach us, and what are your thoughts on them?

"Brothers, my heart's desire and prayer to God for them is that they may be saved. ²For I bear them witness that they have a zeal for

God, but not according to knowledge. ³For, being ignorant of the righteousness of God, and seeking to establish their own, they did not submit to God's righteousness. ⁴For Christ is the end of the law for righteousness to everyone who believes." Romans 10:1-4

Question 5: Romans 10:1 talks about Paul's "hearts desire" for the Jews to be saved. In Romans 10:2, we find that the Israelites have a "zeal for God" but that zeal is "not according to knowledge." What is it that is keeping them from being saved?

☐ They are in bondage to sin and ignoring God's Law.

☐ They are not zealous enough for God's truth as given in God's Law.

☐ Their zeal was not according to knowledge, for they were seeking to establish their own righteousness, based on law-keeping.

Friend, many have a "zeal for God" but might be missing the knowledge of God's righteousness, as found in the gospel message. These Jews had a lack of understanding of the work of the cross and were attempting to establish their own righteousness through law-keeping.

Now please notice what happens when we are lacking in our understanding of the gospel.

"For, being ignorant of the righteousness of God, and seeking to establish their own, they did not submit to God's righteousness." Romans 10:3

Question 6: According to Romans 10:3 what two things happen when we are ignorant of the message of the gospel?

Yes, ignorance of the *"righteousness of God"* found in the gospel of Jesus Christ causes many to seek a righteousness of their own because they did not submit to God's righteousness. Zeal alone isn't enough, and in fact, could be the very thing keeping many from being saved and sanctified. They may not be hearing the message of the cross and combining it with faith in Jesus Christ.

It is critical to share the gospel in living color. That is, to share it over and over from various passages of God's Word. To share the message of the cross and call others to look and see, look, and believe. There isn't another message that needs to be shared from our churches. We have been given the gospel message that is of *"first importance."* When preached, taught, shared, and lived, we are fulfilling the command to "make disciples" in the church and in the world, giving the only message with power to change anyone who hears and believes!

> *"How then will they call on him in whom they have not believed? And how are they to believe in him of whom they have never heard? And how are they to hear without someone preaching?* ¹⁵*And how are they to preach unless they are sent? As it is written, "How beautiful are the feet of those who preach the good news!"* Romans 10:14-15*

> *"For I am not ashamed of the gospel, for it is the power of God for salvation to everyone who believes, to the Jew first and also to the Greek."* Romans 1:16*

Question 7: Please provide your thoughts on this lesson and share what you got out of it, how this might help when sharing the gospel with others?

_____

_____

_____

_____

The Gospel–One Message With Two Parts:
The Resurrection

We're so thankful to have you back today studying the gospel of Jesus Christ with us.

The gospel is the one message Jesus gave to us, to "Go and make disciples" with. This message must be preached and taught in the church then taken into the world to show everyone that Jesus died to forgive their sins, free them from their slavery to sin, and raise them up from the grave. We've seen that we receive "by faith" all that Jesus accomplished while on the cross.

Today, we want to talk about the resurrection and I am excited to be able to celebrate this with you! I hope you're excited about the gospel and the new life we have in Jesus because of His death, burial, and resurrection. The gospel is the very reason the church exists today.

The "good news" of the gospel is one message with two parts:

1. The death
2. The resurrection

> *"For if we have been united with him in a death like his, we shall certainly be united with him in a resurrection like his." Romans 6:5-7*

Question 1: According to Romans 6:5, what are the results of being united with Jesus Christ in His death on the cross? Fill in the blank. If we have been united with Him in death, "we will certainly be _____ with Him in His _____."

Notice from the passage below, the results of uniting, by faith, with Christ in His death:

> *"For if we have been united with him in a death like his, we shall certainly be united with him in a resurrection like his. ⁶ We know that our old self was crucified with him in order that the body of sin might be brought to nothing so that we would no longer be enslaved to sin. ⁷ For one who has died has been set free from sin." Romans 6:5-7*

Question 2: When Jesus died on the cross our "old self" was crucified with Christ. According to Romans 6:6, what is the twofold blessing of being crucified with Christ?

_____

_____

_____

_____

Friend, this is so exciting to see that Jesus died on the cross to remove our sins and Jesus paid our death sentence to do it! Friend, He bore your sins! He was struck but you were healed. He was rejected and sent to die both by men and His Father, but you were accepted and brought near by His blood.

First blessing listed in Romans 6:6: We have been "crucified with Christ" in order that our old man, our sinful nature would cease to exist! Our "body of sin" might be brought to NOTHING!" Think of it, your "body of sin" has been brought to nothing because Jesus' body became sin and was ground down to nothing while hanging on the cross bleeding, as Jesus was gasping for air, yet silent like a lamb led to the slaughter. Your body of sin was paid for through His death on the cross, where you died with Him. Wow, doesn't this make your heart desire to worship, be thankful, and fill you with gratitude?

Second blessing listed in Romans 6:6: The other wonderful thing that happened at the cross is, captives were set free! "...so that we would no longer be enslaved to sin." The cross brings freedom from sin's slavery! Prison doors were opened! Your old man was crucified, buried, and has now risen with Christ so that the body of sin might be brought to nothing and that we would be set free from our SLAVERY to SIN! Now, this is something to celebrate! We should all be singing the Hallelujah chorus! We should all be running, dancing, and singing for such a great salvation!

"For one who has died has been set free from sin." Romans 6:7

Do you see the incredible results of dying with Christ? The one who has died has been "set free from sin." This is truly "good news" for those who die with Christ. It doesn't say that we "might be set free" or that we can "hope to be set free" or that "we will be in recovery for years." NO, it says that the one who has died "has been set free from sin." This is freedom! This is the message that brings good news to the heart of its hearer! This is what changes us from the inside out as the Spirit applies the gospel to the heart! Oh, friend, we are set free when we die with Christ, are buried in the tomb, and raised with power to a new life!

> *"Now if we have died with Christ, we believe that we will also live with him. ⁹We know that Christ, being raised from the dead, will never die again; death no longer has dominion over him. ¹⁰For the death he died, he died to sin, once for all, but the life he lives he lives to God. ¹¹So you also must consider yourselves dead to sin and alive to God in Christ Jesus." Romans 6:8-11*

Question 3: If we have "died with Christ", we believe that we will also live with Him, but how can we live with Him according to Romans 6:9?

☐ If we have died with Christ we will be left behind in a tomb.

☐ If we have died with Christ we will also be raised from the dead.

☐ If we have died with Christ we will never breathe again.

Friend, because Jesus rose from the dead, He can never die again! Death no longer has dominion over Him. Now, *"if we have died with Christ"* we have followed Jesus to the cross, to the grave, and have now been raised up with Him into eternity where we will never die again! This also means that death no longer has dominion over us. We have been raised! Not only is He risen, but we have risen with Him. We were rescued and redeemed through Jesus' shed blood on the cross, and now we are risen and given new life in Him.

> *"For the death, he died he died to sin, once for all, but the life he lives he lives to God." Romans 6:10*

Question 4: When Jesus was hanging on the cross to what did He "die," and who does He "live to" according to Romans 6:10?
- ☐ Jesus died and now lives to please Himself.
- ☐ Jesus died to sin, once for all, and now lives to God.
- ☐ Jesus died and now lives to give you your every desire.

Jesus died to sin! He became sin and then sin was judged in His flesh (Romans 8:3; 2 Corinthians 5:21). Jesus died once! Then He "entered once for all into the Most Holy place, not by means of the blood of goats and calves but by means of his own blood, thus securing an eternal redemption" (Hebrews 9:12).

> *"Since therefore the children share in flesh and blood, he himself likewise partook of the same things, that through death he might destroy the one who has the power of death, that is, the devil, [15]and deliver all those who through fear of death were subject to lifelong slavery." Hebrews 2:14-15*

> *"So you also must consider yourselves dead to sin and alive to God in Christ Jesus." Romans 6:11*

Question 5: As believers in Jesus Christ, that is, in His death for the forgiveness of sins, His burial and resurrection, what "must" we consider ourselves "dead to" and "alive to" according to Romans 6:11?

_____

_____

_____

_____

Yes, we must consider ourselves dead to sin and alive to God through the blood of Christ! Jesus died to sin and lives to God through the resurrection from the dead. Friend, the Christian life is to follow Jesus with our cross held in hand, considering ourselves dead to sin. *"For one who has died has been set free from sin"* (Romans 6:7). We are dead to those sins that held us captive. Dead to the slavery of sin. Dead to the fear of sin. Dead to the fear of death itself because we now live to God.

> *"If then you have been raised with Christ, seek the things that are above, where Christ is, seated at the right hand of God. ²Set your minds on things that are above, not on things that are on earth. ³For you have died, and your life is hidden with Christ in God."*
> *Colossians 3:1-3*

Because we have been raised with Jesus we now have power in our new lives as new creations (2 Corinthians 5:17) to *"seek the things that are above."* The gospel has given us the power to do this. The Spirit enables us to do this now through Christ's death and resurrection! We now have the power within us as new creations to *"set our minds on things that are above"* instead of our former lives when all we could do, as a result of our fallen nature, was set our minds *"on things that are on earth."* Now our minds have been renewed and changed. Our very nature has changed. Our hearts have changed because we have now experienced the power of the gospel in our lives.

"In him also you were circumcised with a circumcision made without hands, by putting off the body of the flesh, by the circumcision of Christ, ¹²having been buried with him in baptism, in which you were also raised with him through faith in the powerful working of God, who raised him from the dead." Colossians 2:11-12

Question 6: What has the cross of Jesus Christ done "without hands" that no human could ever do "with hands" according to Colossians 2:11?

Question 7: We have been buried with Him in baptism and raised in the powerful "working of God." Just how has this happened according to Colossians 2:12?

"...having the eyes of your hearts enlightened, that you may know what is the hope to which he has called you, what are the riches of his glorious inheritance in the saints, ¹⁹and what is the immeasurable greatness of his power toward us who believe, according to the working of his great might ²⁰that he worked in Christ when he raised him from the dead and seated him at his right hand in the heavenly places" Ephesians 1:18-20

Question 8: What is it that needs to be "enlightened" as we hear the gospel, and what do we receive, according to Ephesians 1:18?

_____

_____

_____

Question 9: How much power do we receive, and who receives it according to Ephesians 1:19?

_____

_____

_____

Question 10: How is this *"immeasurable greatness of his power toward us who believe"* connected to the gospel, specifically to the resurrection of Jesus Christ, according to Ephesians 1:20?

_____

_____

_____

At the cross, our *"hearts were enlightened"* so that we "would know" the hope we have in Christ. The riches of his glorious inheritance. The power we have in Christ. The power of His resurrection for those "who believe" the message of Christ! This "immeasurable great power," the same power that raised Jesus from the grave and all the way into heaven where He is seated at God's right hand and His work completed.

LESSON 5:

The Gospel Cuts The Heart!

"Now when they heard this they were cut to the heart, and said to Peter and the rest of the apostles, "Brothers, what shall we do?" Acts 2:37

*D*ear friend, welcome back to the course. In this lesson, we're going to see how the message of the cross "cuts the heart" and therefore the reason we preach Christ crucified! When we preach or teach we must always remember to share the message of the cross because it is the message that has the power to change, reach, cut, and heal the listener's heart.

As you may remember, Acts 2 (quoted above) was the day of Pentecost and the disciples of Jesus were all gathered together in one place (Acts 2:1). And suddenly there came from heaven a sound like a "mighty rushing wind," (Acts 2:2) and it filled the entire house where they were sitting. Divided tongues as of fire appeared to them and rested on each one of them (Acts 2:3). And they were all filled with the Holy Spirit, (Acts 2:4) and everyone heard them declaring the glories of God in their own tongue (Acts 2:2-6) although some thought they were drunk (Acts 2:15). And now speaking, *"filled with the Holy Spirit,"* listen to Peter as he preaches what was uttered through the prophet Joel (Acts 2:16).

"Men of Israel, hear these words: Jesus of Nazareth, a man attested to you by God with mighty works and wonders and signs that God did through him in your midst, as you yourselves know— 23this Jesus, delivered up according to the definite plan and foreknowledge of God, you crucified and killed by the hands of lawless men. Acts 2:22-23

Question 1: According to Acts 2:23, what is the first part of Peter's message?
- ☐ That Jesus was delivered up against God's plan and crucified by good men.
- ☐ That Jesus was delivered up according to God's plan and crucified by lawless men.
- ☐ That Jesus was delivered up but escaped and was never crucified by lawless men.

Yes, the very first words spoken by Peter, who was just filled with the Holy Spirit, was the testimony of the cross of Jesus Christ and Him crucified by lawless men. That this Jesus who was from Nazareth, not to be confused with another Jesus, was *attested to you by God with mighty works and signs that He did before your very eyes*" (Acts 2:22). This Jesus was crucified and killed by lawless men according to the definite plan of God. God planned for His Son to be crucified at just the right time (Romans 5:6) in order to save and set sinners free, even those lawless men that nailed Him to the tree.

Peter continues his preaching…

> "God raised him up, loosing the pangs of death because it was not possible for him to be held by it. ²⁵For David says concerning him, "'I saw the Lord always before me, for he is at my right hand that I may not be shaken; ²⁶therefore, my heart was glad, and my tongue rejoiced; my flesh also will dwell in hope. ²⁷For you will not abandon my soul to Hades, or let your Holy One see corruption. ²⁸You have made known to me the paths of life; you will make me full of gladness with your presence.'" Acts 2:24-28

Question 2: According to Acts 2:27, when Peter was preaching, what did he say happened to Jesus' body?
- ☐ That Jesus was abandoned to the grave and His body decayed.
- ☐ That Jesus was not abandoned to the grave because He was rescued by His disciples.
- ☐ That Jesus was not abandoned to the grave nor did His body see decay.

It was not possible for Jesus to be held by death because He defeated death while on the cross. Jesus' body was not abandoned to Hades nor did God let His Holy One see corruption. Can you hear the passion in Peter's voice as he preaches by the power of the Holy Spirit? Peter is giving testimony of the Son of God, who gave up His life and spirit, and who was laid in a tomb! But Peter states clearly, quoting from Psalm 16:11, that Jesus' body would not see decay, and He would raise to life on the third day!

Peter continues his preaching…

> "Brothers, I may say to you with confidence about the patriarch David that he both died and was buried, and his tomb is with us to this day. [30]Being, therefore, a prophet, and knowing that God had sworn with an oath to him that he would set one of his descendants on his throne, [31]he foresaw and spoke about the resurrection of the Christ, that he was not abandoned to Hades, nor did his flesh see corruption." Acts 2:29-31

Question 3: According to Acts 2:29-31, what was the second part of Peter's preaching, as communicated by the power of the Holy Spirit?

- ☐ That David foresaw and spoke about the resurrection of the Christ.
- ☐ That David foresaw and spoke about the resurrection of himself.
- ☐ That David foresaw and spoke about the resurrection of all believers.

Peter brings his preaching to a close…

> "This Jesus God raised up, and of that we all are witnesses. [33]Being, therefore, exalted at the right hand of God, and having received from the Father the promise of the Holy Spirit, he has poured out this that you yourselves are seeing and hearing. [34]For David did not ascend into the heavens, but he himself says, "'The Lord said to my Lord, "Sit at my right hand, [35]until I make your enemies

your footstool.'" ³⁶Let all the house of Israel, therefore, know for certain that God has made him both Lord and Christ, this Jesus whom you crucified." ³⁷Now when they heard this they were cut to the heart, and said to Peter and the rest of the apostles, "Brothers, what shall we do?" ³⁸And Peter said to them, "Repent and be baptized every one of you in the name of Jesus Christ for the forgiveness of your sins, and you will receive the gift of the Holy Spirit."

Question 4: What happened to this group of men after hearing Peter preach?

- ☐ They were not very impressed because Peter was not a good speaker.
- ☐ They loved the message and made a decision to follow Christ.
- ☐ They were cut to the heart.

Right! When they heard the gospel, they were "cut to the heart." This is why the gospel is the message of "first importance" because it is the only message able to cut the heart and therefore change anyone from the inside out who hears its message. They first heard the message of the gospel (Jesus' death, burial, and resurrection) and we know they heard it and received it "by faith," because the message "cut their hearts."

Now let's notice how the New Testament epistles teach this "cutting", this "circumcision" of the heart for all who believe:

"For no one is a Jew who is merely one outwardly, nor is circumcision outward and physical. ²⁹But a Jew is one inwardly, and circumcision is a matter of the heart, by the Spirit, not by the letter. His praise is not from man but from God." Romans 2:28-29

"In him also you were circumcised with a circumcision made without hands, by putting off the body of the flesh, by the circumcision of Christ," Colossians 2:11

Question 5: What role does circumcision have in "making disciples" in the church through preaching and teaching?

- ☐ The gospel message cuts to the chase and therefore changes the listener's behavior from the inside out making them a good person.
- ☐ The gospel message cuts the heart (without hands) changing the listener from the inside out and fills them with the Holy Spirit.
- ☐ The gospel message cuts the heart and the listener bleeds to death from the inside out.

Friend, when we hear the message of the cross and believe it by faith our hearts are circumcised (cut) "without hands"; meaning this is a work done in the heart by the Spirit of God.

This "cutting" is evidence that you have believed the message of the cross, that "this Jesus" is the one who came to die for you. He bled for you and washed away all of your sin and shame. You were guilty before God due to sin, but He removed all of your guilt on the cross, as Jesus stood in your place. But actually, this Jesus didn't stand in your place, He hung in your place as a criminal, giving up His life so you could have life. Then Jesus gave His spirit so you could receive the Holy Spirit, so you could escape the grip of death and the power of the enemy.

Peter's preaching started with identifying which Jesus he was referring to, He said "this Jesus," the Jesus that was crucified. It was "this Jesus" who was buried but did not see decay. And it was this Jesus who has been raised from the dead and is now seated at the right hand of God.

And in truly believing this message of the gospel, our hearts are cut, wounded and hurt, and are also healed and made whole, while at the same time we receive "the promise of the Holy Spirit."

Friend, did you notice the order? Peter preached a very powerful sermon filled with the Holy Spirit who gave a clear message of the gospel of Jesus Christ: His death, burial, and resurrection. They heard and believed the message "from the heart", and we know they believed from the heart because they were "cut to the heart." This is how we make disciples of all Nations. This is our message we preach from the pulpit, share in Sunday schools, and gather church leaders and elders around. The gospel is the only message that brings hope and has the power to raise up from being dead in sin to becoming alive with Christ. *"So faith comes from hearing and hearing through the word of Christ" (Romans 10:17).*

As we look at Scripture we see this message over and over and it overwhelms our hearts and fills us with new desires, sets us in a new direction, and gives us a new identity in Christ. The cross of Jesus Christ is the anchor for our new life and identity, which is why we must never lose sight of the work Jesus did on the cross for us.

> *"For Christ did not send me to baptize but to preach the gospel, and not with words of eloquent wisdom, lest the cross of Christ be emptied of its power. [18] For the word of the cross is folly to those who are perishing, but to us who are being saved it is the power of God."* 1 Corinthians 1:17-18

In 1 Corinthians 1:17-18, we see that the cross of Christ is powerful in the hearts and lives of all who believe. It's powerful because it is the message that cuts our hearts; that is, it wounds us as it cuts deeply, removing the sin that is bound up in our hearts since birth. This cutting off of our sin, the circumcision of our sin nature is what enables us to begin living for Him who died for us. It is the foundation for a new life lived in holiness and righteousness, the pathway to freedom from sin's dominion.

Question 6: Why is it important that our hearts be cut through believing the message of the cross?

Question 7: You can see from Peter's preaching why the death and resurrection of Jesus Christ are of "first importance." Why is it critical that the church has this one message as its focus? Please share your thoughts.

Circumcised at the Cross

Greetings and welcome back, friend!

In the previous lesson, we saw from Acts 2 that Peter preached the message of the cross and the resurrection of Jesus, and God's Spirit used that message to cut the hearts of those who heard. Through faith in the gospel message, these people whose hearts were cut became disciples of Jesus Christ.

We also saw from Romans 2 and Colossians 2 that all believers are circumcised by the Spirit of God; indeed, this is what makes one a disciple of Jesus Christ.

But how and where does this cutting of the heart happen?

In Acts 2, God used the preaching of the gospel to cut the hearts of those who heard, and today we want to see this truth illustrated with a story from the Old Testament.

Please read the following passage of Scripture and answer the questions below:

"At that time the LORD said to Joshua, "Make flint knives and circumcise the sons of Israel a second time." ³So Joshua made flint knives and circumcised the sons of Israel at Gibeath-haaraloth. (4) And this is the reason why Joshua circumcised them: all the males of the people who came out of Egypt, all the men of war, had died in the wilderness on the way after they had come out of Egypt. (5) Though all the people who came out had been circumcised, yet all the people who were born on the way in the wilderness after they had come out of Egypt had not been circumcised." Joshua 5:2-5

"When the circumcising of the whole nation was finished, they remained in their places in the camp until they were healed. ⁹And the LORD said to Joshua, "Today I have rolled away the reproach

of Egypt from you." And so the name of that place is called Gilgal to this day." Joshua 5:8-9

Question 1: Why did Joshua need to circumcise these people at Gilgal?
- ☐ God's Word was clear that all males had to be circumcised on the 8th day.
- ☐ The children of those coming out of Egypt had not been circumcised yet.
- ☐ Both of the above.

Question :. The Lord told Joshua that something was accomplished through this circumcision at Gilgal; what was it (Joshua 5:9)? "Today I have rolled away the reproach of Egypt from you."

_____

_____

_____

_____

Through this circumcision, God said He had "rolled away the reproach (the disgrace) of Egypt" from them. This reproach refers to their history of slavery to the Egyptians—their past life of bondage as a nation. The Egyptian-identity had been "cut off" and "rolled away" from them, and this moment marked a fresh start for the nation of Israel.

This teaching is instructive for us today. Through our circumcision at the cross, God has "cut off and discarded" our identity as slaves to sin. He has rolled away our shame and disgrace. All our previous labels, indeed all our previous life, have been cut off and rolled away. We have no more labels identifying our sin! Oh what grace He has given us at the cross!

This truth is tremendously important to understand personally and to share with others. We believers must see ourselves as those who have been released from our old life of slavery to sin so that we can fully embrace the new life we have in Christ.

And did you notice where God did this circumcision? Gilgal. The word "Gilgal" means "to roll" or to "roll away." This Hebrew word, Gilgal, has a New Testament counterpart word, which is the word "Golgotha."

> *"So the soldiers took charge of Jesus. [17] Carrying his own cross, he went out to the place of the Skull (which in Aramaic is called Golgotha). 18 There they crucified him and with him two others —one on each side and Jesus in the middle." John 19:16-18 NIV*

When Jesus died on Golgotha, He circumcised all believers (Colossians 2:11). God cut off your sinful self and rolled away your shame and disgrace. He circumcised your entire past identity, removed all your labels, rolled them all away, and buried them in the tomb with Jesus!

Think of this, friend! God has cut off your entire previous life, removed your entire past that is associated with slavery to sin. He has rolled away your dishonor, circumcised your heart, and discarded your disgrace. Oh, how I do praise the Lamb of God Who "takes away the sin of the world" (John 1:29), and with it, all our sinful past and sinful labels! We are "not doing right" if we do not share this good news with our eternal King's household! (2 Kings 7:9)

> **Question 3:** How does this story at Gilgal illustrate what happens as people are shown the cross and come to believe its message?
>
> _____
>
> _____
>
> _____
>
> _____

Let's look again at Colossians 2:11:

> *"In him you were also circumcised with a circumcision not performed by human hands. Your whole self ruled by the flesh*

was put off when you were circumcised by Christ." Colossians 2:11 (NIV)

Question 4: What was circumcised ("put off") at the cross? Fill in the blank. "Your _____ _____ ruled by the _____ was put off when you were circumcised by Christ." Colossians 2:11 NIV

The truth is that at the cross, God circumcised our whole self that was ruled by the flesh. While we still have flesh, we are set free from its domination. While we still have the presence of sin with us, at the cross Jesus broke the power of sin in the life of every believer.

Our circumcision at the cross is significant because it indicates our new identity. This is far different than merely raising our hands or walking an aisle indicating some decision we made, this circumcision shows that we have experienced a dramatic cutting of our hearts, a circumcision of our old nature, a deep and fundamental change in who we are.

The living out of this circumcision in our daily life is a progressive realization, an ongoing experience of the power of the cross. The Bible tells us that we are to now live like who we are, to live in our new identity.

For example, in Ephesians 4:22-24, we are given three specific things we are to do as children of God to live out our identity as those who have been cut in the heart:

- Put off the old self, which belongs to your former manner of life and is corrupt through deceitful desires (Ephesians 4:22). The old person was circumcised at the cross, we are free to discard it.
- Be renewed in the spirit of your minds (Ephesians 4:23). We are to be in the Word, coming often to the cross, asking the Spirit of God to renew our minds. In so doing, we begin to experience the change in thinking that comes from reading and applying the gospel. We are to let the truth of God's Word replace the lies of this world.
- Put on the new self, created after the likeness of God in true righteousness and holiness (Ephesians 4:24).

There is a "change of clothes" that needs to happen with the Christian. We are to put off our old self as we would discard a stinky, old coat; and we are to put on the new person, like a fresh and clean jacket. This is a progressive living out of the circumcised life, so that our very lives become illustrations of what happened at the cross.

Christian leaders are to be like the dressing room attendant at a department store: when we teach, preach or counsel, our role includes helping others take off their old person and put on the new.

> **Question 5:** Thinking through the above three things God tells us to do, which one of them resonates as something significant for you personally?

Dear friend, all believers have been circumcised at the cross of Christ. Our old self who loved to sin, that old nature that was in bondage has been cut off, rolled away, and discarded. *"In him you were also circumcised with a circumcision not performed by human hands. Your whole self ruled by the flesh was put off when you were circumcised by Christ"* (Colossians 2:11 NIV). This happened at the hill of Golgotha, the place of the skull, the cross of Jesus Christ. This made us free in Christ!

Disciples of Jesus Christ are those who have been cut in the heart at the sight of the cross, and who are now learning to live like who we are. We are learning to make our walk match our identity.

Question 6: Are you seeing and believing that the message of the cross is the means of cutting/changing your heart and the hearts of others?

The Spirit Flows From The Cross

"Out of his heart will flow rivers of living water" John 7:38

*E*xperiencing a new heart and life is the evidence of being a true disciple of Jesus Christ. Without a heart transplant, we will never change but will remain the same forever, left with our heart of stone (Ezekiel 36:26) that is "deceitful above all things" (Jeremiah 17:9).

As you will no doubt remember, this heart circumcision is a spiritual one, done without hands (Colossians 2:11), where God removes the evil hard heart and replaces it with a new heart of flesh.

Notice the amazing contrast between the old stony uncircumcised heart and the new heart of flesh. We can see this contrast by comparing Matthew 15:19 with John 7:37-39:

> *"for out of the heart come evil thoughts, murder, adultery, sexual immorality, theft, false witness, slander." (Matthew 15:19)*

> *"If anyone thirsts, let him come to me and drink. Whoever believes in me, as the Scripture has said, 'Out of his heart will flow rivers of living water.'" (John 7:37-38)*

Yes, from out of the old uncircumcised heart come evil thoughts of sinful things, but out of the new heart "flows rivers of living water."

Jesus' death brought us life. A new life. And with this new life, a new heart. A heart that no longer flows out violence, pours out lies, thirsts for sexual immorality, or has murderous thoughts. The river of evil that poured out of our heart of stone for so many years would be circumcised and replaced at the cross as we die with Christ and raise with a new heart, a new life, as a new creation.

> **Question 1:** Please look again at John 7:37-38. What two things need to be done, in order for anyone to experience this amazing change of heart? Please fill in the blanks: "If anyone thirsts, let him _____ ____ ____ and drink. Whoever _____ ____ _____…"Out of his heart will flow rivers of living water."

Yes, it is as we come to Jesus and drink, as we believe in Jesus we experience this flow of the rivers of living water. These happen at the cross of Jesus Christ (John 6:54).

> **Question 2:** According to John 7:37-38, What would "flow out" and where would it flow from?
> ☐ Rivers of life would flow out of our works of righteousness.
> ☐ Rivers of healing water would flow out of our lives.
> ☐ Rivers of living water would flow out of our hearts.

Yes! Those coming to Jesus and believing in Him would have their thirst quenched and rivers of living water would flow out of their hearts. Jesus is pouring His thirst-quenching water into you and me when we "come to Him" and "believe in Him" and what pours out of us is *"rivers of living water."*

This is the life of the believer who has come to the cross and has looked and seen Jesus, the *"man of sorrows"* nailed to the tree, becoming a curse. They have seen Him become thirsty while fighting for them on the cross, pouring out His life unto death, yet able to quench the thirst of those who come and believe.

Friend, the heart of the believer is one that has received and then pours out to others what he himself has received. We see this illustrated when Paul said, "For I delivered to you as of first importance what I also received" (1 Corinthians 15:3). And the Thessalonians "welcomed the message" of the cross, and then the message "rang out from them" (1 Thessalonians 1:6-8).

The gospel of Jesus Christ always comes to us and then pours out of us like a river to others. We are no longer broken cisterns (Jeremiah 2:13) or stagnant and broken water sources, but like a flowing fountain of life where rivers of living water pour into us from the cross and flow out of our new hearts into the lives of others.

> "...and hope does not put us to shame, because God's love has been poured into our hearts through the Holy Spirit who has been given to us." Romans 5:5

Isn't this incredible? God's love through the gospel of Jesus Christ has been "poured into our hearts." Once our hearts were cut and healed from hearing and believing the gospel, God's love would now pour into us through the work of the Holy Spirit which he has given us. We believed that Jesus purchased us with His own life on the cross to buy us out of the market of slavery, He gave us a new heart and put a new spirit in us (Ezekiel 36:26).

> "If anyone thirsts, let him come to me and drink. [38]Whoever believes in me, as the Scripture has said, 'Out of his heart will flow rivers of living water. [39] Now this he said about the Spirit, whom those who believed in him were to receive, for as yet the Spirit had not been given, because Jesus was not yet glorified." John 7:37-39

Question 3: What event(s) took place before the Spirit could be given according to John 7:39?
- ☐ His death and reincarnation, because Jesus was not yet justified.
- ☐ His death and resurrection, because Jesus was not yet qualified.
- ☐ Jesus' death and resurrection took place because Jesus was not yet glorified.

Question 4: The rivers of living water refers to the Spirit not yet given. Who would receive the Spirit?
- ☐ Those who believed in Him would receive the Spirit.
- ☐ Those who did good works would receive a good return.
- ☐ Those who waited patiently would be lifted up.

Oh friend, please see what changes would be made. As you think about the Holy Spirit flowing from new hearts, consider these questions: what happened to the murderous thoughts? What happened to the false witness? What happened to the sexual immorality? What happened to the slander, theft, and murder?

With our new hearts of flesh, the evil that once flowed out of our hearts would be crucified and buried! We would then be raised up with Christ where the rivers of living water given through the Spirit would flow out of our hearts. Instead of evil flowing out of our old hard hearts, our new hearts would flow the rivers of living water of love, joy, peace, patience, kindness, goodness, faithfulness, gentleness, and self-control (Galatians 5:19-23)

I've got a river of life flowing out of me
I've got a river of life flowing out of me
Makes the lame to walk and the blind to see,
Opens prison doors, sets the captives free
I've got a river of life flowing out of me.[1]

Friend, receiving the Spirit that flowed into our hearts from believing the message of the cross, makes the lame walk and the blind see. Our prison doors are opened wide and captives are set free. This is the life Jesus died to give you and me and the cross is the message of hope and power that radically changes our lives and gives us the ability to truly love like never before.

Question 5: Are you seeing how the Spirit flows from the cross and does the work in us? Please share your thoughts.

---

1   River of Life, L. Casebolt

Question 6: Have you had your thirst quenched by coming to Jesus' cross and believing in Him? Are you experiencing the "rivers of living water" flowing out of your heart? If not, what do you need? Please share.

_____

_____

_____

_____

And did you notice the Scripture says "rivers" of living water rather than a "river" of living water? Can you imagine this incredible change and exchange from evil coming out of our hearts to receiving the Spirit and now what comes flowing out is; love, joy, peace, patience, kindness, goodness, faithfulness, gentleness, and self-control (Galatians 5:19-23)

Here's an illustration from the Old Testament that clearly shows how the Spirit flows from the cross of Jesus Christ.

> *"All the congregation of the people of Israel moved on from the wilderness of Sin by stages, according to the commandment of the Lord, and camped at Rephidim, but there was no water for the people to drink. 2 Therefore the people quarreled with Moses and said, "Give us water to drink." And Moses said to them, "Why do you quarrel with me? Why do you test the Lord?" 3 But the people thirsted there for water, and the people grumbled against Moses and said, "Why did you bring us up out of Egypt, to kill us and our children and our livestock with thirst?" Exodus 17:1-3*

Question 7: What were the people complaining about? Please list as many things as you can here:

_____

_____

_____

_____

"So Moses cried to the Lord, "What shall I do with this people? They are almost ready to stone me." ⁵ And the Lord said to Moses, "Pass on before the people, taking with you some of the elders of Israel, and take in your hand the staff with which you struck the Nile, and go. ⁶ Behold, I will stand before you there on the rock at Horeb, and you shall strike the rock, and water shall come out of it, and the people will drink." And Moses did so, in the sight of the elders of Israel."

Question 8: What was the Lord's solution to the quarreling, demanding, and complaining of the Israelites? Please share.

_____

_____

_____

_____

The Israelites were quarreling and complaining in the wilderness. Here is their sinful condition clearly displayed:

- The people quarreled with Moses
- They demanded water
- They tested the Lord
- They questioned the Lord. "Why did you bring us up out of Egypt?"

- They charged the Lord with doing evil. *"To kill us and our children and our livestock with thirst?"*
- They were ready to stone Moses

But notice the amazing solution! The one solution for the thirst, demanding, and quarreling of the Israelites (their sin) was to strike the rock, and water would come out of it for the people to drink.

Dear friend, Jesus is The Rock that was struck (1 Corinthians 10:4), and His very life was opened up on the cross and poured out for you and I. Jesus bled from His head, His hands, and His feet. From His side, water and blood flowed to cleanse, forgive, remove our sin, wash and quench our thirst. The cross is the fountain opened up, it is where we can drink and our thirst will finally be satisfied and our sins forgiven (Zechariah 13:1).

The cross is where all of our sins are met in one place, and they were all crushed in Jesus' flesh. As He was poured out like water on the cross (Psalm 22:14) He satisfies the thirst of those who come to the cross, look to Jesus and believe in Him. *"and all drank the same spiritual drink. For they drank from the spiritual Rock that followed them, and the Rock was Christ"* (1 Corinthians 10:4).

Question 9: Please share your thoughts about Jesus, The Rock that was struck, His very life poured out to death to quench the thirst of The Church with the Spirit.

_____

_____

_____

_____

"...but whoever drinks of the water that I will give him will never be thirsty again. The water that I will give him will become in him a spring of water welling up to eternal life." John 4:14

This is how lives are forever changed. This is how hard hearts that once had evil lodged in them are set free by the love Jesus poured out on the tree. And this is how we reach The Church with the good news of the gospel of Jesus Christ. The cross has the power to change hearts, forgive sins, free us from sin's power, enabling us to receive the river of living water within us through the Spirit He has given us.

The Spirit and The Cross

"Let me ask you only this: Did you receive the Spirit by works of the law or by hearing with faith?" Galatians 3:2

To some, the gospel may be something that just needs to be heard once, or maybe once in a while. Others may feel like they've already made the decision to follow Jesus so the gospel is not necessarily for them, but for the lost. And others have "moved on to more mature things"; like learning how to live out the commandments of God personally in their lives.

There are many different thoughts about the gospel in the church today. Even using the term "gospel" has lost its meaning, and therefore its power. Many have attempted to live out their Christian life by "good works" and by "doing their best." But friend, we need to set our sights squarely on the gospel and its power to free captives! For it is the message that changes us from who we were–to who we are in Christ.

Let's take a look at what we see in our churches today and the absolute difference the gospel makes.

Those who rely on the law; trying to "do good" works in their own power by obeying the commandments of Jesus. Focusing on their studies and/or accomplishments they've made while attending Bible College or Seminary and how they're growing in them and in their knowledge of Scripture.

"But we know that it is impossible for us to obey the law apart from the work of the cross and the Spirit. "Look: I, Paul, say to you that if you accept circumcision, Christ will be of no advantage to you. ³ I testify again to every man who accepts circumcision that he is obligated to keep the whole law. ⁴ You are severed from

Christ, you who would be justified by the law; you have fallen
away from grace" (Galatians 5:2-4).

Those who rise up from within; teaching a "different gospel" that does one of two things:

First, it throws the flock into confusion. Those who might have heard the gospel have become confused through "a different gospel", and therefore have not understood the power of the real gospel personally for themselves.

Secondly, these same ones rise up to take away disciples after themselves. While scattering and confusing church members as outlined in lesson 1, their objective is to teach a different gospel and gain followers. "*I am astonished that you are so quickly deserting him who called you in the grace of Christ and are turning to a different gospel— 7 not that there is another one, but there are some who trouble you and want to distort the gospel of Christ*" (Galatians 1:6-7).

Those who have experienced power; or are beginning to experience the "power of God" in their lives (Romans 1:16).

Even if their lives are changing slowly, they can see a change within their own heart and are seeing Jesus changing their desires. They are experiencing love and forgiveness in their hearts. They are talking about how they are experiencing power in their lives and learning to "walk by the Spirit" and not in the flesh that has held them captive. The cross has given them grace and mercy, and the love of God is being flooded into their hearts. They are really sensing what it means to be a new creation in Christ. They are beginning to experience that Jesus has cut their heart by His Spirit, and cut their iron chains of sin through the message of the cross, and is now bringing them out of their grave of death, darkness, and despair.

Dear friend, the gospel of Jesus Christ is the power of God! This power of God is not found by relying on man or obeying the law, but by seeing the One who died so that we can be transformed into His very image (Romans 8:29; 2 Corinthians 3:18). The gospel has the power to change anyone who believes, and whoever believes in his heart the message of the cross will never be the same!

"O foolish Galatians! Who has bewitched you? It was before your
eyes that Jesus Christ was publicly portrayed as crucified. 2 Let me

ask you only this: Did you receive the Spirit by works of the law or by hearing with faith? 3 Are you so foolish? Having begun by the Spirit, are you now being perfected by the flesh?" Galatians 3:1-3

Question 1: What was the first thing the bewitched Galatians needed to hear in order for their lives to be made right again according to Galatians 3:1?
- ☐ That it was before your eyes that Jesus Christ had slipped away into the night.
- ☐ That it was before your eyes that Jesus Christ was publicly speaking.
- ☐ That it was before your eyes that Jesus Christ was publicly portrayed as crucified.

Question 2: How did the Galatians receive the Spirit, and what specifically did they hear according to Galatians 3:2?
- ☐ By hearing with faith the message of Jesus' crucifixion on the cross.
- ☐ By hearing with faith the message of Jesus being a carpenter.
- ☐ By hearing with faith the message that Jesus was from Nazareth.

Notice how Galatians 3 begins with Jesus Christ being "publicly portrayed as crucified" right before their eyes. This is how and why they received the Spirit–when they believed the message of the cross. It was in taking their eyes off of the cross that they had become "foolish Galatians" who began to walk according to the flesh.

"Are you so foolish? Having begun by the Spirit, are you now being perfected by the flesh?" Galatians 3:3

Question 3: What is it that makes believers "foolish" after receiving the Spirit and believing the message of Christ crucified?

_____

_____

_____

_____

When we hear the message of the cross and believe it by faith, like the Galatians, we begin a new life where we receive and are then led by the Spirit (Galatians 5:16). When we continue to look to Jesus and the work of the cross, continuing to believe it's message, we will not fall back into being "perfected by the flesh." This was the foolishness of the Galatians, and any believer who takes their eyes off of Jesus Christ and Him crucified.

Friend, the cross is where the power is, the power to change our lives and the power to keep us. I'm not saying that we will never sin again or fall again. But what will be needed when that happens? Yes, just like the Galatians needed to look to the crucified Christ to bring them out of their foolishness of walking in the flesh, we likewise look to the cross that puts to death the flesh and keeps us in step with the Spirit (Galatians 5:25).

> *"Did you suffer so many things in vain—if indeed it was in vain?*
> *⁵ Does he who supplies the Spirit to you and works miracles among you do so by works of the law, or by hearing with faith—*
> *⁶ just as Abraham "believed God, and it was counted to him as righteousness"? Galatians 3:4-6*

Question 4: What about you, friend, have you received the Spirit by hearing the gospel of Jesus Christ only to return again to the law to begin walking in the flesh? Please share:

_____

_____

_____

We see that the Spirit was received by faith by those who heard the message of the cross. This is the same way in which we receive the Spirit today, hearing by faith. But it is also the message we are to keep looking to so we do not fall back into walking in the flesh.

> *"Does he who supplies the Spirit to you and works miracles among you do so by works of the law, or by hearing with faith—"*
> *Galatians 3:5*

Question 5: What is the connection between the two statements, "who supplies the Spirit to you" and "works miracles among you?

- ☐ When we receive the Spirit we still need to obey every command in the Bible.
- ☐ When we receive the Spirit we see the miracle of transformation in us where we are becoming new creations in Christ.
- ☐ When we receive the Spirit not much happens because we still desire to walk in the flesh.

When we look at the cross and believe the message we receive the Spirit. He then "works miracles among us." That is, we become new creations. We become focused heavenward instead of having our minds set on the flesh and the things of earth. We experience the miracle of walking by the Spirit rather than walking by the flesh and the law (that never had the power to change us or set us free). *"But you will receive power when the Holy Spirit has come upon you, and you will be my witnesses in Jerusalem and in all Judea and Samaria, and to the end of the earth"* (Acts 1:8).

> **Question 6:** When we preach and teach the gospel, "that Jesus Christ was publicly portrayed as crucified", some will hear, believe and receive the Spirit which will create a "new creation" miracle in them.
> ☐ True
> ☐ False

> *"For we know, brothers loved by God, that he has chosen you, 5 because our gospel came to you not only in word, but also in power and in the Holy Spirit and with full conviction. You know what kind of men we proved to be among you for your sake."* 1 Thessalonians 1:4-5

> **Question 7:** How can we know that the Thessalonians had been chosen by God?
> ☐ Because the gospel came to them in word, but lacked the power of the Holy Spirit, and had no conviction.
> ☐ Because the gospel came to them in word, in the power of the Holy Spirit, and with full conviction.
> ☐ Because the gospel never came to them, so that had no power of the Holy Spirit, and they were not under conviction.

Do you see it? It was the message of the gospel that came "not only in word" but it also came "in power" and in the "Holy Spirit" and with "full conviction." Friend, the message of the cross is not a weak insurance policy to "keep you from God's wrath" or to "get you into heaven." NO! It is power that comes to radically change the human heart. This was the first message the Holy Spirit spoke through Peter in Acts chapter 2.

Look now with me to see the results of what happened to the Thessalonians upon hearing the message of the gospel.

"And you became imitators of us and of the Lord, for you received the word in much affliction, with the joy of the Holy Spirit, 7 so that you became an example to all the believers in Macedonia and in Achaia. 8 For not only has the word of the Lord sounded forth from you in Macedonia and Achaia, but your faith in God has gone forth everywhere, so that we need not say anything." 1 Thessalonians 1:6-8

Friend, the Thessalonians became "imitators" of those who shared the gospel message, and of the Lord Himself! They received the message in much affliction and yet with joy in the Holy Spirit. This is what happens to those who hear and believe the message of the cross. Their lives are changed from serving idols to imitating the messengers, so much so that they themselves "became examples" to ALL the believers in Macedonia and Achaia!

Wow! Are you seeing the gospel's power to change? And finally, in verse 8, we see that the Thessalonians' faith has gone forth everywhere! Oh, friend, this is the hope and power of the gospel that changes the life and direction of those who receive the message, *"for you received the word in much affliction, with the joy of the Holy Spirit."*

"For they themselves report concerning us the kind of reception we had among you, and how you turned to God from idols to serve the living and true God, 10 and to wait for his Son from heaven, whom he raised from the dead, Jesus who delivers us from the wrath to come." 1 Thessalonians 1:9-10

Question 8: When the gospel came in the power of the Spirit, what were the results when the Thessalonians received the word in verse 9?
- ☐ The gospel turned them "to idols" and away from God to serve them.
- ☐ The gospel could not turn them "to God" because it did not come to them with power.
- ☐ The gospel turned them "to God" from idols to serve the living and true God.

Do you want to know how to become free from the idols of impurity, gluttony, laziness, depression, and more? The gospel is so powerful when preached and taught, received and believed, that it "turns us to God" and "from idols."

Testimonies and The Power Of The Cross!

*W*elcome back, friend!

Today, we're going to jump right into two testimonies from students who have experienced the power of the cross, where they died with Christ, were buried, and were raised to life. The purpose of these testimonies is to show how intimately connected the message of the cross is with the transforming power of the Spirit. These are testimonies that display the power of God (Romans 1:16) where we will see how the work of Jesus Christ crucified, "supplies the Spirit to you and works miracles among you" (Galatians 3:5).

AMANDA WRITES: "I COULD BE A POSTER CHILD FOR HORROR STORIES of psychiatric drugs. All glory goes to God, but much in part thanks to Setting Captives Free, I have been "drug-free" for over two years now.

I was first put on anti-depressants when I was 12 years old, and this began a series of in and out-patient hospital stays, "counseling" sessions (many horror stories here as well from secular counseling), many diagnoses, and a lifestyle filled with habitual sin of all kinds. For over ten years, I dealt with eating disorders, cutting, suicidal thoughts, and so much more. Doctors diagnosed me with severe depression, Oppositional Defiant Disorder (ODD), Obsessive-Compulsive Disorder (OCD), multiple personalities (this diagnosis came from a "Christian counselor" at a "Christian" college I was attending at the time), Borderline Personality Disorder, Bi-Polar Disorder, and so much more.

I took so much medication over the years that I lost count. The drugs that I remember being on at one time or another include Effexor, Seroquel, Risperdal, Paxil, Valium, Lithium, Zoloft, Lexapro, Prozac, Wellbutrin, and Trazodone. There are more I'm sure, but these are the ones I remember. I also had medications to help "contain" the side effects of these drugs. It was crazy. They used to say the drugs worked better "alongside" one another. What foolishness! One of my last doctors said there might not be much more for me to try; he offered electric shock therapy.

An important note, looking back I can see that God allowed me to step away from the "medication lifestyle" when a church I was attending wanted to help wean me off and turn me to Christ for full strength as well. My psychologist at the time was quick to point out that she had another patient they tried to "work with" who wound up back in the hospital. She labeled the church a cult and quickly got my mom on board to sweep me out of this church and "harm's way."

Now, as an adult, I'm grateful that God has given me this second chance for freedom from psychotropic medications, but I am not naive to the fact that many will oppose the idea of freedom. Prescription drug use is something that has become so common and accepted even within the "Christian" community, and that seriously disturbs me.

Since I had been on so many drugs for so many years, I was very used to the "get on/drop off" process. I was familiar with most of the dosages and the side effects I would be experiencing as well. Even though I knew what was coming with side effects, etc., it was still a challenging time, but God used it for good to help grow my faith and dependence upon Him.

At Setting Captives Free, I learned to apply biblical principles to my life. First, I had to check my motives. Did I really want to get off meds so that I could live a life glorifying to God? Or was it just because I wanted to be "normal"? Next, I had to come to a point where I knew and believed that the sacrifice Christ made for me was enough so that I could "Trust in the Lord with all my heart and lean not on your own understanding." (Proverbs 3:5) Even though I trusted that Jesus could save me from other sins, I still had in the back of my mind (from years of "therapy") that this was one area of my life that 'couldn't be "fixed" by God. I even had some counselors teach that God was using these drugs to "help me." But now I know better. When I placed my trust in Christ, I knew that He could save me…even in this area, and it 'didn't matter what anyone else said.

I had to repent from this sin of unbelief, from the belief that Jesus couldn't save me from this area. Then I had to turn and trust. I had developed a lot of bad habits, like running to cutting or suicidal thoughts when times were hard.

I learned to replace these wrong thoughts and actions with the cross-centered truth. I learned how to think biblically. Hebrews 3:13 says, "But encourage one another daily, as long as it is called Today, so that none of you may be hardened by sin's deceitfulness." So, I dove into the Word of God, feasting on the Scripture daily.

My husband encouraged me along the way. During times of great distress (as I suffered from the sickness and despair of the med drop-off), my husband would lay his hands on me and pray for me. I had accountability online as well as with an older woman in our church. I called or wrote many times when I felt like I was drowning, and they pointed me to Jesus, who carried me through. I utilized the free biblical counseling provided by our church as well, and this also helped to identify some of my unbiblical thought patterns.

I learned to cling to the promises I found within the Bible, and ultimately, God's Word has set me free. A key verse for me has been 2 Corinthians 12:9 which says, "But he said to me, 'My grace is sufficient for you, for my power is made perfect in weakness.' Therefore I will boast all the more gladly about my weaknesses, so that Christ's power may rest on me."

Over time, as the medications cleared my system and the Word of God reoriented my mind, my thoughts became clear and stable. I came to see myself how God saw me, as a child of God. I am comforted by Psalm 139:14, which says, *"I will praise you because I am fearfully and wonderfully made…"* When I am tempted, I remember I Corinthians 10:13, *"And God is faithful; he will not let you be tempted beyond what you can bear."*

I'm not going to lie to you, life is not always easy, but once you get into a habit of running to the Word of God, you will find as I have that Jesus can provide comfort that can't be found anywhere else. As 2 Corinthians 10:5 says, "…take captive every thought to make it obedient to Christ."

Whenever a thought came to mind that I know was not glorifying to God, I would immediately run to a Scripture verse. I even made "memory cards" by placing some relevant Scripture I knew I should memorize onto note cards and then I kept them in my purse so they'd be handy wherever I was. Eventually, I had the verses memorized, and I immediately turned my thoughts to the promises of the Scripture whenever I had an unbiblical thought. I repeated Psalm 46:1 many times throughout the day, *"God is my refuge and my strength, an ever-present help in trouble."* Another one of my favorite verses found in

Philippians 4:8, which says, *"Finally, brothers, whatever is true, whatever is noble, whatever is right, whatever is pure, whatever is lovely, whatever is admirable—if anything is excellent or praiseworthy—think about such things."*

I do my best to handle each day as it comes. Matthew 6:34 says, "Therefore do not worry about tomorrow, for tomorrow will worry about itself. Each day has enough trouble of its own." I got outside of myself by looking for ways to help others starting by simply befriending someone at church who needed help. God didn't intend for us to be "lonely," he intended for us to serve others. Matthew 20:28 says, *"just as the Son of Man did not come to be served, but to serve…"*

I knew and understood that God did not guarantee me a perfect life full of peace and harmony. 1 Peter 3:15 says, *"Always be prepared to give an answer to everyone who asks you to give the reason for the hope that you have."* If you never have times where you're in the "valley," why would you need a reason to hope? When God helps you overcome that valley, however, then you can tell others and "give an account" of an amazing Redeemer who truly saves, and that has been my experience - to God be the glory!

I no longer believe in being on medicine for life, like I had several "doctors" tell me I would need. 2 Corinthians 12:9 says, *"But he said to me, "My grace is sufficient for you, for my power is made perfect in weakness." Therefore I will boast all the more gladly about my weaknesses, so that Christ's power may rest on me."* I believe this with all of my heart. His grace is sufficient in every area of my life, including the arena of my mind. John 15:5 says, *"apart from me, you can do nothing."* I take this to heart, and I cherish my time in His Word.

I seek to arm myself for the daily battle that this life can be. Ephesians 6:10-13 says, *"Finally, be strong in the Lord and in his mighty power. Put on the full armor of God so that you can take your stand against the devil's schemes. For our struggle is not against flesh and blood, but against the rulers, against the authorities, against the powers of this dark world and against the spiritual forces of evil in the heavenly realms. Therefore, put on the full armor of God, so that when the day of evil comes, you may be able to stand your ground, and after you have done everything, to stand."* I do this by praying, reading and studying His Word, and doing my best to live "do all for the glory of God."

I have been off all meds for several years now. Some may have been tempted to say that I have such a good life I wouldn't have cause for "depression" and therefore have no need for any meds anymore. However, my life is full of challenges: my husband has been out of a job for over a month now, and we have two little blessings (a four and a three-year-old), who love to "challenge" me on a daily basis. But God's grace is still sufficient. I have a peace I didn't have two years ago. I believe the Holy Spirit has provided a *"peace that transcends all understanding."* He is my refuge, my strength, and my hope, and I thank God every day for saving my life and my family. To God be the glory, forever and ever, Amen!"

> **Question 1:** Please share your thoughts about Amanda's testimony and how it was the message of the gospel that changed her life.

HERE'S OUR SECOND TESTIMONY **FROM IRIS**:

"Depression makes sure it is felt, seen, heard, smelled, tasted. Depression doesn't stay an acquaintance. It fights to make its presence known. It is felt in blows to the head and cuts to the wrists. It is seen in everyday tasks left undone. It is heard in loud cries and sad music. It is smelled in dirty clothes and burnt suicidal letters and tasted in binge foods, and pills.

Depression is not passive; it is assertive, forceful, and pushy. It whispers into your ear in convincing and manipulative ways. It holds your hand down the street while you cross with your eyes closed. It shows you the way to an abandoned building and while you're there hands you a piece of broken glass to relieve your pain. It tells you to hang up on the suicide hotline to prevent them from judging you.

Depression pretends to be your friend. It tells you to stay in bed and rest, but it says the same thing every morning. It tells you to turn your phone off after you send a suicidal text message. It tells you to hide in closets, cars, and public restrooms while everyone else is having fun at a party because it isn't safe out there. It tells you to walk out of class and church service. It tells you to treat yourself but says the same thing when you have $10 left for the week.

In 2017, I cut and harmed myself again. I wrote suicidal letters, went to two different counselors, and took antidepressants. I also had terrible eating habits; I was either not eating or always eating. Depression took over most of my year. It made me lonely, angry, joyless, fearful, and insecure. Prevented attachment and built walls.

Depression was and is stubborn, strong, and clingy, but it wasn't and isn't indestructible.

During my first week as a college student, I decided to make Jesus Lord of my life. But depression has been a part of my life since I was a kid. So when I felt feelings of despair, I would beat myself up for not understanding Paul's command to "Be joyful always."

When was God going to restore the joy of my salvation? Why was my soul downcast? If Jesus came to bring me joy and asked me to remain in Him to make my joy complete, why wasn't I joyful? Maybe I wasn't truly a disciple? But I was holding on to his teachings. Even if I couldn't muster the strength to read, I would listen to the Bible. I would pray all day long. I was opening up; I was even getting professional help. Why was I so miserable?

I notice it now, but I didn't then; I was so self-focused. All of the above questions revolve around me. As if my happiness and my joy were what this world is about, but it wasn't, it isn't, and it will never be about me.

God places us in the times and places we need to be so that we will seek Him. He placed me in a church that is devoted to God and each other, and I am so grateful. When I step back and take my eyes off of myself, I see everything God was doing and keeps doing to heal me.

I recall how one of the ladies at church came up to me and said she had noticed that I hadn't been myself lately, and she knew something that could help me. We didn't get to talk then, but a couple of weeks later she showed me Isaiah 61 and explained how a course at Setting Captives Free had helped her with her purity when she was in college.

I thought it would not help because it was just a website. What could I possibly learn that I already don't know? Be still? Encourage others? Pray more? Read more? Know Satan's lies? I thought I was doing everything already, but I decided to give it a try.

I signed up for the course and asked to have a mentor, and the first time I read her feedback and how she was praying for me, I bawled. God put more people to fight with me. People that understand and have overcome!! New hope!!

I quickly realized that the course was all about going back to the cross where Jesus defeated sin, insecurity, loneliness, shame, guilt, depression, and all evil, where he disarmed Satan, where he switched His fine garments with my filthy clothes, where he took my place so that I would no longer have to be a prisoner captive of her sin, depression, and anxiety.

Many of the Scriptures I read I had already read. I had looked at the cross before; I thought I already knew that story, but that was the point. I was looking at it like an old movie that I had watched millions of times. I thought the cross had nothing new to offer. But, oh, I was so wrong!

The cross is the center of Christianity. Without the cross, there would be no hope. The whole Bible revolves around Jesus and the cross. It was the ultimate sacrifice. It was the answer to everything, including depression.

There were many days where the lessons were too much for me because it meant that I had to look at the cross. I didn't want to look at the pain I put Jesus through! I was surprised every time I had doubts or questions, and when I would finally decide to do the next lesson, God's word would calm my anxious heart. I learned to look at everything through the eyes of Jesus and the cross.

This journey was hard. I had to surrender daily. And I learned that I will always have to do that. To wake up and look at the snake that was conquered and killed, now on a pole, defeated. To look at my defeated sin, to look at Jesus becoming my sin so that I could be made righteous. Jesus took it all. He became my sin. And so now my sin is gone. He rose, and now he lives in me.

The cross taught me that it is never about me. That when I take my eyes off of the cross, off of Jesus and what he already finished, it gets depressing. If I look at the snake that bites, I cannot be healed. But if I run to the pole and look up, it heals me. It is ugly. It is painful. It is healing. It is hope. The cross is where I get a new life free of depression. One where the focus is on HIM, where there is joy in what he has accomplished, where sin no longer rules, where there is freedom, where there is Jesus."

Question 2: Please share your thoughts on Iris's testimony and how it was the gospel that rescued and transformed her life.

_____

_____

_____

_____

Setting Captives Free literally receives thousands of testimonies every year from both men and women who are experiencing freedom from slavery to impurity (pornography and all forms of sexual impurity), but this next testimony comes from a wife of a man who found freedom. Here is her testimony:

ANNA WRITES, "I FOUND THIS COURSE OVER TWO YEARS AGO. AT that time, I was busy with a betrayal trauma support group, so I decided I didn't need this material. Fast forward two years, and in pain and anger, I said to my husband, "There is no way out of this for me. I will be trapped in this pain forever. You should have thought this through and thought about me before deciding to go down this path. There is no healing from this. I just have to learn to survive it and live the rest of my life in pain." That is where I was when I started A United Front 30 days ago. I was angry, bitter, and filled with hate. I was lost in my pain and was losing hope of it ever getting better.

I learned through this course that I was focusing on the wrong thing - my pain. My focus needed to be where true hope and healing are found - Jesus Christ. I started this course with a huge weight. Little by little, the beauty of Christ and His work on the cross was revealed to me. I was learning how I betrayed Christ, and how He loved me so much He rescued me. I was learning lessons on forgiveness, humility, patience, and taking my thoughts captive. There were so many practical and powerful lessons. At each stop on the way, I was able to drop a little bit of the pain I was feeling. Each day the weight was getting lighter and lighter as I was learning the truth of Jesus Christ and who I was in Him. I was able to see myself and my husband accurately. I was no longer the "good one," and he the "bad one." We were both sinners in a battle fighting together for our marriage. And I can clearly see my husband is not my enemy.

Thirty days ago, I started this course as a bitter, angry woman being crushed under the weight of pain, but I'm leaving this course a kinder, more compassionate woman filled with the love and hope of Christ. My husband said it best the other day when he said, 'it's so nice to see you smile and laugh again.'

I recommend this course. If you are considering this course, please know that hope is not lost. This course will help. I had tried trauma groups, counseling, and was no better off, but the Gospel is powerful and life-changing. Who better to go to for help and healing than the One who created you and died on the cross to rescue you."

> **Question 3:** Please share your thoughts about Anna's testimony and how it was the message of the gospel that changed her life.

Friend, the point of this lesson is to show the amazing transforming message of the cross brings the supernatural power of the Spirit to work miracles. May the church return to making this message of first importance (1 Corinthians 15:1-4); of teaching, preaching, and counseling from the cross!

Gospel Application In Mentoring (Discipling)

oday, we wanted to illustrate why we share the gospel with every one of our students, the results the gospel has in every situation and how it is the answer to every spiritual problem and question. Please notice how the student below changed from, being "defeated," to having his "burden lifted," and shifting from wanting to "win arguments" to instead sharing "Christ crucified."

Below is the interaction between a Setting Captives Free student and his mentor.

Student writes, "I feel so tired and defeated now...Jehovah's Witnesses came to my gate - lovely people - but what a frustration. How can we get the truth through to them if they think the same of us? How can they be convinced? And then they probably think, how can we be convinced? What does one do???!!!"

Mentor writes, "_____, you are going to be shocked when you read my answer. We "lift up the cross" and allow the Spirit to apply the gospel to the heart. As you remember Peter preached the gospel (that the Jesus they crucified actually died for their sins and then rose on the third day) and immediately following these words were recorded for us, *"Now when they heard this they were cut to the heart, and said to Peter and the rest of the apostles, "Brothers, what shall we do?"* (Acts 2:37). Share the gospel for it is the antidote for everything and everyone! The gospel changes the heart and mind. The gospel is where we find forgiveness and hope. It is where we meet our own death and resurrection."

Student writes, "So you are saying that even with JWs, the best offense/defense is just the gospel. Let the Spirit carry it to their hearts instead of winning the argument. Let the Spirit do the talking through the gospel? Let the hearer listen or not?"

Mentor writes, "You got it, brother! Just yesterday, I was talking with a dear friend of mine, and he was sharing his frustration about his family. I told him that he should love those who do not deserve our love, as God loved us, sending His Son to die while we were sinners (Romans 5:8).

During this conversation, the mentor shared how his family will only be united with the love of Christ in the gospel. Living in the flesh separates people because it always desires its own way; however, the death and resurrection of Jesus Christ always unites, because, at the cross, our flesh is put to death in Christ!

Later, after the meeting, the student sent this in a group text, "I always get edified, encouraged and redirected when you guys show me the cross, and how it applies." This is how sharing the gospel affected one heart. The only way anyone can be saved, sanctified, edified, redirected, encouraged, etc., is sharing the gospel–the power of God (Romans 1:16).

Our merely human arguments will leave the captive chained up and hopeless. We may walk away excited that we "won an argument" and can now boast "in the flesh," while our hearers walk away still "dead in sin" (Ephesians 2:1) and without hope! But if we had shared the gospel instead of attempting to "win an argument" they could have at least walked away with a "seed in their heart," or maybe even be "cut to the heart" and healed by the wounds of Jesus!!!"

Student writes, "The power of God unto salvation. That's 'all' it takes, and yet it took God everything. We should not get in the way with our own arguments. Let the gospel pierce the heart. What more can we do, but just that. Thank you, brother. In fact, even learning to share just the gospel is another burden the Lord lifts from us. In the end, it all comes down to Christ and Him crucified."

Question 1: What was the initial condition and concern of the student?

Question 2: What made the difference in this conversation between the student and his mentor?

_____

_____

_____

_____

Question 3: What was the student's conclusion of the conversation?

_____

_____

_____

_____

Question 4: Do you have any additional thoughts about this exchange between the student and his mentor? Please share them here.

_____

_____

_____

_____

Below is a response from one of our mentors after the above interaction was shared in a weekly check-in for Setting Captives Free mentors.

Joce writes, "It was simply stunning to see his heart transformed from being defeated to preaching the gospel back to you! All by the Spirit applying the gospel and testimony you shared. I loved his added insight: "even learning to share just the gospel is another burden the Lord lifts from us". Isn't it wonderful that sharing the gospel is mutually encouraging? (Romans 1:12)

> *"We do not preach about ourselves, but we preach that Jesus Christ is Lord and that we are your servants for Jesus. God once said, "Let the light shine out of the darkness!" This is the same God who made his light shine in our hearts by letting us know the glory of God that is in the face of Christ." 2 Corinthians 4:5-6*

As mentors we do not elevate ourselves or use persuasive arguments which only change the mind and not the heart. For it is the gospel we want our students to delight and depend on:

"It is better to trust in the LORD Than to put confidence in man." Psalm 118:8 We present the gospel in each of the Setting Captives Free lessons so that our student's heads, by His Spirit, will lift, turn and face this wondrous place of the bloodstained cross where transformations of the heart happens.

We are showing each student what the gospel means, we are telling them how it affects us personally in our own hearts, we are sharing what has happened to us and to others because of it! We are singing, praying, reading, listening and rejoicing about the gospel with each student all with one message "Come over here! Look at the Crucified Christ - go nowhere else for here is the solution for your struggles. Not in looking at your 'selves', or the mentor, or in the world's programs, philosophies or reasonings, or in any man or woman for the answers."

When we preach that Jesus Christ is Lord and His death and resurrection, we look into the wonderful face of Christ and we behold the glory of God Himself. His light shines into the darkness of people's hearts bringing clarity out of confusion, giving liberty to the captives, the recovering of sight to the blind and oppressed - all who are who are downtrodden, bruised, crushed, and broken down by calamity (Luke 4:18 AMPC).

To ourselves as mentors, as well as to our students, we say in so many ways: SEE your sin bearing, wrath absorbing, death defeating substitute at the cross! SEE the bleeding sacrifice of the Lamb of God. SEE your sins hanging on His disfigured body. SEE Jesus loving you by dying for each sin, and SEE Him rising with resurrecting, earth shaking power lifting you out of the pit! SEE the extraordinary love of One Man Who gave His all for you so you could be ushered into an everlasting life of grace and intimacy with God, with a new, tender, forgiven heart that melts with awe and wonder at the mention of His Name!"

> *"Sing to the LORD, praise his name; proclaim his salvation day after day." Psalm 96:2*

> **Question 5:** Please share your thoughts on Joce's writing and how the gospel has the power to transform us.

We hope that you've seen how critical it is to stay committed to the gospel message itself and not being sidetracked by another message. We remain focused on Jesus' death and resurrection as we share, preach, teach and counsel anyone in need with this most powerful message. May the church and its members, the body of Christ, *rediscover the power of the cross!*

The Gospel Equips For The Work Of Ministry

When the gospel of Jesus Christ has cut, crushed, cured our hearts and set our lives and desires in a new direction–which at one time we thought impossible—we desire to share this good news of victory and freedom we experience at the cross with others.

When we experience the gospel's power like this we begin to share with the world, the "good news" that Jesus died and rose in victory over sin and death on the third day. This message makes disciples, sets captives free and brings all who have ears to hear and eyes to see into a right relationship with God, thereby building up the body of Christ, the church.

Today we'll study together how it is the gospel which propels and prepares the church to "Go and make disciples": sending "apostles, the prophets, the evangelists, the shepherds and teachers" (Ephesians 4:11) with the same message of hope and power that Jesus accomplished through His death and resurrection. Let's begin by looking at a passage in Ephesians chapter 4.

> *"But grace was given to each one of us according to the measure of Christ's gift. ⁸ Therefore it says, "When he ascended on high he led a host of captives, and he gave gifts to men." ⁹ (In saying, "He ascended," what does it mean but that he had also descended into the lower regions, the earth? ¹⁰ He who descended is the one who also ascended far above all the heavens, that he might fill all things.) ¹¹ And he gave the apostles, the prophets, the evangelists, the shepherds and teachers, ¹² to equip the saints for the work of ministry, for building up the body of Christ, ¹³ until we all attain*

to the unity of the faith and of the knowledge of the Son of God, to mature manhood, to the measure of the stature of the fullness of Christ, ¹⁴ so that we may no longer be children, tossed to and fro by the waves and carried about by every wind of doctrine, by human cunning, by craftiness in deceitful schemes. ¹⁵ Rather, speaking the truth in love, we are to grow up in every way into him who is the head, into Christ, ¹⁶ from whom the whole body, joined and held together by every joint with which it is equipped, when each part is working properly, makes the body grow so that it builds itself up in love." Ephesians 4:7-16

Question 1: What is the purpose the Lord gave "the apostles, the prophets, the evangelists, the shepherds and teachers" according to Ephesians 4:12?

☐ To use 12-step groups for the work of ministry, for building up the body of Christ.

☐ To equip the saints for the work of ministry, for building up the body of Christ.

☐ To equip the church with programs, for building up the body of Christ.

Question 2: Looking at Ephesians 4:7-10, what message are the apostles, the prophets, the evangelists, the shepherds and teachers supposed to proclaim that "equips" and "builds up the body of Christ"?

☐ The death and resurrection of Jesus Christ (that Jesus "descended" to the cross for our sins, and "ascended" to the throne on the third day).

☐ The death of God the Father but the resurrection of Christ.

☐ The death and the resuscitation of Jesus Christ.

All believers are to have this same singular focus, that is, to become equipped for the work of gospel ministry. All believers are to "make disciples of all nations" with the good news of Jesus' death and resurrection for the forgiveness of sins and the transformation of lives. The gospel is "for building up the body of Christ."

As a bodybuilder would use the components offered to him at the gym for "building up his body," believers have been given the gospel–for building up the body of Christ. The church body must be built up before we are able to go out and reach the world. In other words, the gospel message must be firmly taught and preached in the church before the church is able to take it into the world.

As we deliver this powerful message of the cross, God sees to it that more and more are added to the "body of Christ," thereby building it up. We are not to be merely about "adding numbers," but rather we are to be showing people that Jesus died for them, removed their sin from them, and therefore destroyed its power over them with His blood.

We want all people to see Jesus breathing out His last breath to give them His Spirit, taking their sin on Himself and dying, and cleansing them with His blood. In dying like this, Jesus is drawing all people out of darkness and into His marvelous light where they experience the power of His death and resurrection themselves, and begin to proclaim the excellencies of God.

> *"But you are a chosen race, a royal priesthood, a holy nation, a people for his own possession, that you may proclaim the excellencies of him who called you out of darkness into his marvelous light." 1 Peter 2:9*

Friend, Jesus first descended into death on the cross before being raised from the dead where He ascended on high to set captives free. "*When he ascended on high he led a host of captives, and he gave gifts to men*" (Ephesians 4:8). Jesus entered into this dark world, into the darkness of death to rescue you and bring you "into his marvelous light."

> *"For since, in the wisdom of God, the world did not know God through wisdom, it pleased God through the folly of what we preach to save those who believe. ²² For Jews demand signs and Greeks seek wisdom, ²³ but we preach Christ crucified, a stumbling block to Jews and folly to Gentiles," Colossians 1:21-23*

Apostles, prophets, evangelists, shepherds, and teachers were given the same message to preach, Jesus Christ and Him crucified. This message is a stumbling block to some, foolishness to others, but to those being saved—THE POWER OF GOD (1 Corinthians 1:18). The gospel is for the church!

> **Question 3:** Are you a pastor, elder, or church leader equipping your church members with the message of the cross? Are you a church member being equipped with the message of the cross? Please share your thoughts.
>
> _____
>
> _____
>
> _____
>
> _____

"He said to them, "Go into all the world and preach the gospel to all creation" (Mark 16:15).

"...until we all attain to the unity of the faith and of the knowledge of the Son of God, to mature manhood, to the measure of the stature of the fullness of Christ," Ephesians 4:13

> **Question 4:** According to Ephesians 4:13 what is the faith and knowledge that unites and matures believers?
>   ☐ The knowledge of the Bible and how many books are in it.
>   ☐ The knowledge of the Son of God and the work Jesus did as a carpenter.
>   ☐ The knowledge of the Son of God and the work Jesus did on the cross.

Until "we all attain the unity of faith." Isn't it amazing Jesus' death and resurrection is the message both of "equipping", "building," and where we "attain the unity of faith?" It is the knowledge of the Son of God, and the love of the Son of God where we find maturity and stability. Specifically, it is Jesus' death and resurrection that binds us together in "perfect love" and "unity."

"You yourselves like living stones are being built up as a spiritual house, to be a holy priesthood, to offer spiritual sacrifices acceptable to God through Jesus Christ" (1 Peter 2:5).

So far we've seen that the apostles, the prophets, the evangelists, the shepherds, and teachers were all given the responsibility of sharing the death and resurrection of Jesus Christ for the following reasons:

- To equip the saints for the work of ministry for Christ
- To build up the body of Christ
- To attain to the unity of the faith in Christ
- To attain to the knowledge of the Son of God
- To mature manhood in sanctification through Christ
- To the measure of the stature of the fullness of Christ

"so that we may no longer be children, tossed to and fro by the waves and carried about by every wind of doctrine, by human cunning, by craftiness in deceitful schemes." Ephesians 4:14

Question 5: Please fill in the blanks. "...____ _____ _____ may no longer be _____, tossed to and fro by the waves and carried about by every _____ of _____, by human cunning, by _____ in _____ _____" Ephesians 4:14

This is how the message of Jesus' death stabilizes all believers so that we are "no longer tossed" to and fro by the "waves" and "carried by winds" of doctrine, but stabilized as we are anchored to the cross. Children are those who are tossed to and fro by the waves and carried by every wind of doctrine.

This also shows the instability we have outside of the gospel of Jesus Christ. Like a ship going to and fro and tossed about by the waves, so is the instability of our lives without the stabilizing power found in the death of Christ which "anchors our souls" (Hebrews 6:19), so that we are not blown around by the waves and carried by the winds of other doctrines.

Other teachings (doctrines) are inferior to the gospel message because they do not proclaim specifically Jesus Christ crucified and risen for the forgiveness of sins—where God's power resides (Romans 1:16; 1 Corinthians 1:18). The teaching of the cross equips, builds up the body, unites believers in unity of faith, unites us in the knowledge of the Son of God, bringing us to maturity through sanctification, and fills us to the full measure of Christ. As Galatians 1:11 says other doctrines become "man's gospel" where The Gospel that "saves and sanctifies" takes a back seat by human cunning and craftiness in deceitful schemes which indeed is "another gospel" (Galatians 1:8).

> *"For I am jealous for you with the jealousy of God himself. I promised you as a pure bride to one husband—Christ. ³ But I fear that somehow your pure and undivided devotion to Christ will be corrupted, just as Eve was deceived by the cunning ways of the serpent. ⁴ You happily put up with whatever anyone tells you, even if they preach a different Jesus than the one we preach, or a different kind of Spirit than the one you received, or a different kind of gospel than the one you believed"* 2 Corinthians 11:2-4 (NLT)

> *"Rather, speaking the truth in love, we are to grow up in every way into him who is the head, into Christ,"* Ephesians 4:15

Question 6: What causes us to "grow up" in every way into Christ, the head?
- ☐ Speaking the truth whether they like it or not!
- ☐ Speaking the truth in love.
- ☐ Speaking the truth by nicely pointing out people's sin and shaming them.

Rather than living like children who are tossed to and fro and carried by winds of other doctrines we should rather, "speak the truth in love and grow up in every way into Him who is the head, into Christ."

If we are speaking the "truth in love" we are manifesting the fruit of the Spirit and walking in the power and love of the Spirit. The same message that God uses to save, sanctify and send us into the world to proclaim, is the same message of love that builds up and stabilizes the church. As we are speaking the truth in love to one another we grow up together into the love of Christ.

> *"But the fruit of the Spirit is love, joy, peace, patience, kindness, goodness, faithfulness," Galatians 5:22*

Jesus spoke the truth in love to us by laying down His life, forgiving our sins, tasting death, paying the penalty of our sin, and sealing the fate of all who believe with the gift of the Holy Spirit. Jesus did not come with a rod of correction or pointing His finger in judgment at us, rather He gave His whole body on the cross where He spoke the truth in love to us with His arms opened wide and His hands nailed to the cross, shedding His blood in love for us.

> *"For God so loved the world, that he gave his only Son, that whoever believes in him should not perish but have eternal life" (John 3:16). He was crucified, but we live. He was punished, but we are set free. He was crushed, but we are made whole. "You have come to Jesus, the one who mediates the new covenant between God and people, and to the sprinkled blood, which speaks of forgiveness instead of crying out for vengeance like the blood of Abel" (Hebrews 12:24 NLT).*

> *"from whom the whole body, joined and held together by every joint with which it is equipped, when each part is working properly, makes the body grow so that it builds itself up in love." Ephesians 4:16*

> *"Therefore, brothers, since we have confidence to enter the holy places by the blood of Jesus, [20] by the new and living way that he opened for us through the curtain, that is, through his flesh, [21] and since we have a great priest over the house of God, [22] let us draw near with a true heart in full assurance of faith, with our hearts sprinkled clean from an evil conscience and our bodies washed with pure water." Hebrews 10:19-20*

"And he is before all things, and in him all things hold together. [18] And he is the head of the body, the church. He is the beginning, the firstborn from the dead, that in everything he might be preeminent. [19] For in him all the fullness of God was pleased to dwell, [20] and through him to reconcile to himself all things, whether on earth or in heaven, making peace by the blood of his cross." Colossians 1:17-20

Without the work Jesus accomplished through His death and resurrection we would have no hope. No message to proclaim. No change of heart. No disciples made. No new creation experience. No peace by the blood of the cross.

Question 7: Please share your final thoughts of Jesus, whose blood was shed for the church to equip us, build us up in love, unite us in love, stabilize and mature us.

_____

_____

_____

_____

The Gospel and Forgiveness

"Be kind and loving to each other, and forgive each other
just as God forgave you in Christ." Ephesians 4:32 (NCV)

Today we're going to study why we should forgive "just as God forgave you in Christ." We'll see how the cross is the key that unlocks the door to forgiving others. As we are looking to the cross, we should first ask, "how have I been forgiven"? Secondly, "how can I forgive others the way I've been forgiven?"

Friend, this is the message we share, that Christ loved us and has forgiven all our sins, even the ones the world may deem as unforgivable. When we see just how much we've been forgiven, looking at the sacrifice Jesus made for us and the price He paid for us on the cross, our hearts are moved within us! We are filled with awe and wonder that every sin we've ever committed has been put onto Christ and put to death in Christ. Jesus loved us all the way to death on a cursed cross, which moves and motivates us to extend forgiveness to others the way we've been forgiven, even to anyone who has sinned horribly against us.

Question 1: In Christ, our sins have been forgiven, canceled, buried, and removed. For what sins has Jesus forgiven you? Please list them.

_____

_____

_____

_____

Please study through with me through the following passage:

> "A woman in that town who lived a sinful life learned that Jesus was eating at the Pharisee's house, so she came there with an alabaster jar of perfume. [38] As she stood behind him at his feet weeping, she began to wet his feet with her tears. Then she wiped them with her hair, kissed them, and poured perfume on them. [39] When the Pharisee who had invited him saw this, he said to himself, "If this man were a prophet, he would know who is touching him and what kind of woman she is—that she is a sinner." [40] Jesus answered him, "Simon, I have something to tell you." "Tell me, teacher," he said. "Two people owed money to a certain moneylender. One owed him five hundred denarii, and the other fifty. [42] Neither of them had the money to pay him back, so he forgave the debts of both. Now which of them will love him more?" [43] Simon replied, "I suppose the one who had the bigger debt forgiven." "You have judged correctly," Jesus said." Luke 7:37-43 (NIV)

Question 2: According to the above story, even though the debts were far from "equal," whose debt was forgiven and canceled?
- ☐ Only the one with the smaller debt was forgiven.
- ☐ Neither one, they still owed the debt.
- ☐ He forgave and canceled the debt of both.

"Now, which of them will love him more?"

Friend, the more we are forgiven, the more love will be flowing from our hearts. Why? Because we see the mountain of sin and debt we owed to God but could not pay. Then we see Jesus stepping in and paying a debt He did not owe. We see Him walking up the mountain where He crushed our mountain of sin in His flesh on that cross! We owe our very lives to Him because our mountain of sin was reduced to nothing. We know it should have been us on that cross, paying our debt, but not one of us had the means by which to pay what was owed.

Notice that one owed "five hundred denarii," and the other only owed "fifty." It didn't matter the size of the debt, both were extended forgiveness, and their debts were canceled just as Jesus' death was enough to cleanse and forgive even the largest of sin debts. No one can "sin too much," or "out sin" God's grace because God's grace in Jesus Christ is far greater!

> *"The law was brought in so that the trespass might increase. But where sin increased, grace increased all the more," Romans 5:20 (NIV)*

Do you see it, friend, "Where sin increased," God's "grace increased ALL THE MORE."

> **Question 3:** How grateful are you in seeing your mountain of sin "wiped out" and "canceled" on Calvary's hill where Jesus put ALL your sin, sinful past, and future sins to death in His flesh?

> *"Then he turned toward the woman and said to Simon, "Do you see this woman? I came into your house. You did not give me any water for my feet, but she wet my feet with her tears and wiped them with her hair. 45 You did not give me a kiss, but this woman, from the time I entered, has not stopped kissing my feet. 46 You did not put oil on my head, but she has poured perfume on my feet. 47 Therefore, I tell you, her many sins have been forgiven—as her great love has shown. But whoever has been forgiven little loves little." 48 Then Jesus said to her, "Your sins are forgiven." Luke 7:44-48 (NIV)*

Friend, do you see the focus of this woman? She's not looking at herself and all the sins she's committed, but at her Savior, weeping at His feet, seeing and sensing the love and forgiveness to her personally and she was deeply affected by it. Why? Because ALL HER SINS have been forgiven! She's not finding her identity in her sins, but in her Savior who forgave ALL her sin debt. Whether it was "five hundred denarii" or "five million denarii" worth of sin her heart was free and filled with love as she was being loved by Jesus. The fact that she is "loving much" is a result of her seeing and knowing how much she's been loved and forgiven by Jesus.

> **Question 4:** Can you see how much you've been loved and forgiven? That neither you or this woman could not "out sin" the grace of God, as the blood of Jesus increased (flowed) all the more? Please share your thoughts.

_____

_____

_____

_____

Look now with me at the cross and see all of your sins upon Christ. Are there many sins for which you have been forgiven? Then let the love of Jesus Christ fill you to overflowing just like it did with this woman who loved much and wiped her tears with her hair at Jesus' feet. Or maybe you see that you have been forgiven little by Jesus, "whoever has been forgiven little loves little" (Luke 7:47). In other words, if we want to "love much" we need to see that we've been "forgiven much" through Jesus' sacrifice. Friend, keep looking to the sacrifice of Jesus Christ, contemplating just what it cost Him and how He humbled Himself, became nothing, emptied Himself and died for you.

Debt canceled! PAID IN FULL! You are forgiven! Oh, may this cause your heart to be overjoyed! May you run and not grow weary! May you sing and shout for joy! May you serve Him will all your heart! Please do not fall into the trap so often heard, "I can forgive, but I'll never forget." This is not how we are forgiven in Christ at the cross! Through Jesus' death, our sins are "blotted out" NEVER TO BE REMEMBERED again!

"I, even I, am he who blots out your transgressions, for my own sake, and remembers your sins no more." Isaiah 43:25 (NIV)

"...as far as the east is from the west, so far has he removed our transgressions from us." Psalm 103:12 (NIV)

Question 5: What has God removed from you and forgotten?
- ☐ God removes but remembers my sin.
- ☐ God often reminds me of my sin so that I will remain humble.
- ☐ God has removed and forgotten my sin through Jesus' death/resurrection.

Think about this for a moment with me. How would it make you feel if someone constantly brought your past sins to mind, reminding you how much you've hurt them, followed by, "I've forgiven you, but I'll just never forget!"? There can be no genuine forgiveness if there's a "but" involved in the transaction of forgiveness.

In the Luke 7 passage we're studying today, we see the following contrast between Simon and the sinful woman:

Then he (Jesus) turned toward the woman and said to Simon:

- I came to your house, but you did not give me any water for my feet (v44)
- I came to your house, but you did not give me a kiss (v45)
- I came to your house, but you did not put oil on my head (v46)

Then he (Jesus) turned toward the woman and said to Simon:

- But she wet my feet with her tears and wiped them with her hair (v44)
- But this woman, from the time I entered, has not stopped kissing my feet (v45)
- But she has poured perfume on my feet (v46)

"Therefore, I tell you, her many sins have been forgiven—as her

great love has shown. But whoever has been forgiven little loves little." Then Jesus said to her, "Your sins are forgiven." Luke 7:47-48 (NIV)

The only words Jesus said directly to the woman in this story were, "Your sins are forgiven." This woman is the one who owed the larger debt, the one who owed the "five hundred denarii" and whose sins "were many." Now she was free and forgiven, loving the One who would go to the cross and carry all her sins and sorrow to die a man of sorrows for her. Oh, friend, have you seen Jesus dying for you, pleading on your behalf with His nail-scarred hands because of His great love for you? (Ephesians 2:4)

> *"When the Pharisee who had invited him saw this, he said to himself, "If this man were a prophet, he would know who is touching him and what kind of woman she is—that she is a sinner." Luke 7:39 (NIV)*

Earlier, we saw a contrast between Simon and the sinful women, but now we see a contrast between Simon and Jesus. Simon saw this woman as a "sinner," but Jesus said to her, "Your sins are forgiven." Jesus saw her as pardoned of punishment and free from accusations, knowing He would soon be accused in her place and take her punishment on Himself! Friend, can you see Jesus turning towards you saying, "your sins are forgiven"?

What Jesus said about this woman could be summed up in Isaiah's experience as well. Read the following passage, keeping the forgiven woman's experience in mind:

> *"And I said: "Woe is me! For I am lost; for I am a man of unclean lips, and I dwell in the midst of a people of unclean lips; for my eyes have seen the King, the Lord of hosts!" [6] Then one of the seraphim flew to me, having in his hand a burning coal that he had taken with tongs from the altar. [7] And he touched my mouth and said: "Behold, this has touched your lips; your guilt is taken away, and your sin atoned for." [8] And I heard the voice of the Lord saying, "Whom shall I send, and who will go for us?" Then I said, "Here I am! Send me." Isaiah 6:5-8*

This is the message we preach in the church, teach in the church and reach out to the world with. Imagine this woman (or anyone affected deeply by the gospel) coming and sharing her testimony at your church. Sharing the love of Jesus that has deeply affected her heart and therefore her life. Sharing with tears how much she's been loved and forgiven at the cross. How she's found help and a home, her dwelling in Christ.

As the church preaches the cross for the forgiveness of sins in Jesus' shed blood, may we hear more and more testimonies of this incredible love, as people see and receive the love of Jesus and become filled with overflowing love for others.

Though our sins are many and run deep, Jesus' love went even deeper into the depths of death for us. Jesus removed our guilt and sin by shedding His blood and atoning for them on the cross. At the cross, "your guilt is taken away, and your sin atoned for" as Jesus suffered at the burning altar of the cross under God's wrath—dying as if He were the one who sinned—as if He were the guilty one.

"Be kind and loving to each other, and forgive each other just as God forgave you in Christ." Ephesians 4:32 (NCV)

Question 6: Please fill in the blanks. "Be kind and _____ to each other, and _____ each other just as God _____ you in Christ." Ephesians 4:32 (NCV)

Question 7: How has this lesson reminded you to forgive as you've been forgiven and love as you've been loved?

_____

_____

_____

_____

Biblical Forgiveness

*I*n previous lessons, we discussed the importance of forgiving others as the Lord has forgiven us.

> *"Bear with each other and forgive one another if any of you has a grievance against someone. Forgive as the Lord forgave you."*
> *Colossians 3:13 (NIV)*

We mentioned one definition of forgiveness, which is that God chooses to remember our sins no more.

> *"No longer will they teach their neighbor, or say to one another, 'Know the Lord,' because they will all know me, from the least of them to the greatest. 12 For I will forgive their wickedness and will remember their sins no more." Hebrews 8:11-12 (NIV)*

Question 1: According to Hebrews 8:11-12, how do people come to know the Lord?
- ☐ They raise their hand, walk the aisle, and pray the sinner's prayer.
- ☐ They come to know the Lord through the forgiveness of sins.
- ☐ They obey the law, especially the Ten Commandments.

Hebrews 8:11-12 teaches us that we come to know the Lord through the forgiveness of our sins. When we turn to the cross and see that Jesus loved us enough to die for our forgiveness, it lets us know the character of God and receive the love of God. We come to know God as a forgiving God, a God who pardons (Isaiah 55:7), a God who refuses to remember our sins so that we can have a relationship together.

And as we experience this forgiveness, relishing that God chooses never to remember our sins, we now know how to forgive those who sin against us. It's not that God has a bad memory; instead, it's that He deliberately chooses not to remember our sins.

The imperative we have as children of God is to forgive others as God has forgiven us, which means that we forgive and choose not to remember the wrongs done against us. Do you frequently recall or think about offenses that someone said or did to you? If yes, this could be an indication that you have not forgiven your offender.

If you are in the position of leadership in your church, you must help others see their full pardon at the cross! As they see their complete forgiveness through Jesus' blood shed on their behalf, and they understand that God refuses to remember their wrongs, they will be empowered to forgive and intentionally not remember the wrongs of others and avoid the trap of bitterness.

> *"Love is patient, love is kind. It does not envy, it does not boast, it is not proud. It does not dishonor others, it is not self-seeking, it is not easily angered, it keeps no record of wrongs." 1 Corinthians 13:4-5 (NIV)*

In this lesson, we want to add to this definition of forgiveness, so that we can not only rejoice in God's forgiveness of us through Christ but also understand and know how we are to forgive others as God has forgiven us.

Biblical forgiveness means:

First, as stated in the previous lesson and summarized above, God chooses not to remember our sins against Him (Hebrews 8:11-12).

Second, God chooses to pay the price.

To truly forgive someone as God has forgiven us, we also must pay the price.

Bill Miller, one of the board members of Setting Captives Free, uses this illustration to explain this aspect of forgiveness:

"Let's say that you are my employee, and while I was out one day, you saw $50.00 cash laying on my desk; temptation overtook you, you stole the money and immediately spent it on yourself. But then your conscience began to trouble you, and you felt compelled to confess your theft to me. But the problem is, the money is gone, and you are unable to replace it.

In this case, if you ask me to forgive you, it means I'm out $50.00. If I say I will forgive you, I am paying the price of that forgiveness. It cost me something to forgive you. Now you might, over time, be able to repay me, but at the moment of your confession, forgiveness means I willingly pay the price to forgive you."

Friend, this is one of the great things that happened at the cross: Jesus Christ paid the price of our sin. "*The wages of sin is death*" (Romans 6:23), and Jesus paid that price, and all who believe stand before God forgiven, which means we do not owe God for our sin. The immense price, the blood of God Himself (Acts 20:28) was shed, Jesus was pierced and wounded and beat, the price was paid, the debt is gone, we are free! And Jesus did this willingly! "*The reason my Father loves me is that I lay down my life—only to take it up again. No one takes it from me, but I lay it down of my own accord*" (John 10:17-18).

When Jesus completed the work of redemption on the cross, just before He gave up His Spirit, He cried out in a loud voice, "*It is finished!*" Found only in the Gospel of John, the Greek word translated "it is finished" is telelestai, which is an accounting term that means "paid in full." When Jesus cried out those words, He was preaching the gospel! He was communicating that He wiped away our sin debt owed to His Father entirely and forever. And there is no way we could ever repay Jesus for this price He paid, and what's more, He doesn't even want us to try. God never requires nor allows repayment from us.

And this is how we forgive those who sin against us. Sin always incurs a debt, but as those who have received abundant forgiveness from God, we follow Christ, forgive and pay the price, whether that is actual money or in another way. By contrast, we don't require our offender to "work it off," we don't require a "pound of flesh" or cling to a need to see our offender suffer. Instead, we remember the cross of Christ, where He suffered, and forgive others as God has forgiven us.

If you are a Christian counselor, one of your primary roles will be to help people to 1) experience the forgiveness of God themselves, and 2) teach them how to forgive others as God has forgiven them not in word only but indeed and in truth (1 John 3:18).

> **Question 2:** How does God choosing to pay the price of forgiveness cause you to value the work Jesus did on the cross?

_____

_____

_____

_____

Third, God does not treat us as our sins deserve.

> *"He will not always accuse, nor will he harbor his anger forever;*
> *10 he does not treat us as our sins deserve or repay us according*
> *to our iniquities." Psalms 103:9-10 (NIV)*

God did not always accuse us, at the cross, He directed His accusation and condemnation to Jesus. He did not harbor His anger forever but poured it all out on His Son, who stood in the place of all sinners. Now, when God forgives, He refuses to treat us as our sins deserve. The reason is, He treated Jesus as our sins deserve. So, now He treats us as His Son deserves.

What a glorious truth that is powerful to change our hearts and lives! We rebelled against God, we spurned His love, we chose our sinful way, lived to gratify our lusts, and yet in forgiveness, God refuses to treat us as our sins deserve. Rather, our relationship with Him is based on grace! Grace purchased at the cross with the precious blood of Jesus! Amazing grace that goes on forgiving even when sin abounds in our lives.

"We all, like sheep, have gone astray, each of us has turned to our own way, and the Lord has laid on him the iniquity of us all." Isaiah 53:6 (NIV)

"The law was brought in so that the trespass might increase. But where sin increased, grace increased all the more" Romans 5:20.

"Then Peter came to Jesus and asked, "Lord, how many times shall I forgive my brother or sister who sins against me? Up to seven times?" Jesus answered, "I tell you, not seven times, but seventy-seven times" Matthew 18:21-22.

Because Jesus Christ purchased grace for us at such an expensive price, His own life's blood, God can, and does, officially treat us only according to grace, never according to our sins.

Now we see how we are to forgive others: we are to refuse to treat them as their sins deserve. We are to forgive them over and over, again and again just as God forgives us.

If you are leading others in your church, you must help them understand that God does not treat them as they deserve to be treated, and for this reason, they are not to treat others who perpetrate wrongs against them as they deserve.

Tough love mantras such as "Kick them to the curb" and "Throw them out until they straighten up," are not according to the gospel, but rather natural principles taught by the world.

> **Question 3:** Please give an example of a time when it would be "natural" to treat an offender as he deserves to be treated.

Question 4: Reflect on your answer to Question 3 and consider how the message of the cross encourages us to treat sinners differently than would be "natural." What are your thoughts?

Fourth, God does not repay us according to our sins.

This aspect of biblical forgiveness is similar to God not treating us as our sins deserve, and yet we can add to this that God does not take "revenge" of any kind. God is not only loving and forgiving, but He is also just. He cannot repay us according to our sins because He already poured out all His wrath for our sins on Jesus. On the cross, God loaded Jesus up with the sins of the whole world, and then poured out His wrath and put Him to death. God "repaid" Jesus, not us. Now, God repays us according to what Jesus did. Jesus lived righteously and loved perfectly, and God repays us for Jesus' righteous living and perfect loving.

> *"He is the atoning sacrifice for our sins, and not only for ours but also for the sins of the whole world." 1 John 2:2 (NIV)*

> *"Consequently, just as one trespass resulted in condemnation for all people, so also one righteous act resulted in justification and life for all people." Romans 5:18 (NIV)*

The "one righteous act" that Jesus did, going to the cross in full obedience to His Father, justified all people who believe in Him and gave them life through His death. Here we see how we are to treat others, never taking revenge, only loving them as if they had lived a perfect life toward us as if they had loved us perfectly.

If you are preaching the message of the cross regularly, it is essential to show people that God will never come after them in revenge, even for their horrendous crime of crucifying His Son. Likewise, we believers must learn never to take revenge on others, but to forgive as God forgives us.

> *"When they hurled their insults at him, he did not retaliate; when he suffered, he made no threats. Instead, he entrusted himself to him who judges justly. [24] "He himself bore our sins" in his body on the cross, so that we might die to sins and live for righteousness; "by his wounds, you have been healed." 1 Peter 2:23-24 (NIV)*

> *"Do not take revenge, my dear friends, but leave room for God's wrath, for it is written: "It is mine to avenge; I will repay," says the Lord. [20] On the contrary: "If your enemy is hungry, feed him; if he is thirsty, give him something to drink. In doing this, you will heap burning coals on his head." [21] Do not be overcome by evil, but overcome evil with good." Romans 12:19-21 (NIV)*

Wow, this is hard to do, right? The truth is, it is "impossible to do!" And yet this is the very thing God does for us, repaying Jesus for our sins and repaying us for Jesus' righteous living. He will never repay us for our sins, and to forgive others means we will never take revenge on them.

> *"God made him who had no sin to be sin for us so that in him we might become the righteousness of God." 2 Corinthians 5:21 (NIV)*

> *"I delight greatly in the Lord; my soul rejoices in my God. For he has clothed me with garments of salvation and arrayed me in a robe of his righteousness, as a bridegroom adorns his head like a priest, and as a bride adorns herself with her jewels." Isaiah 61:10 (NIV)*

Question 5: Please explain why God will never take revenge on you.

_____

_____

_____

_____

In summary, we have studied the following aspects of biblical forgiveness:

- First, God chooses not to remember our sins.
- Second, God pays the price for our sins.
- Third, God does not treat us according to our sins.
- Fourth, God does not repay us according to our sins.

If you have embraced the cross as the reason why God treats us differently than our sins deserve, then you know that to live the cross out in your life is to forgive as you have been forgiven.

Question 6: After reading the truth of the gospel in this lesson, have you seen a need to treat anyone differently than you have been doing? Please explain:

_____

_____

_____

_____

Note: Biblical forgiveness does not mean that we ignore sin or permit ongoing abuse of any kind. Crimes such as substance abuse, physical violence, or any other illegal activity should be reported to the civil authorities. Habitual sin issues should be handled according to the principles given in Matthew 18:15-20.

The Wedding and the Wine—
the Body and the Blood

When thinking about the Gospel and the Church, we must remember that we, the church, are the bride of Christ because Jesus purchased us with His own blood. All believers are, in this life, "engaged to be married" and will one day celebrate the "Marriage Supper of the Lamb" (Revelation 19:19).

Right now, as people who are "engaged," we look to Jesus for love, comfort, enjoyment, and fellowship, rather than to this world for those things. In this lesson, let's see the glorious truth that Jesus is our Bridegroom who gave His life to make us His own (Ephesians 5:22-33) and how He began to reveal His glory at a wedding.

> *"On the third day, a wedding took place at Cana in Galilee. Jesus' mother was there, and Jesus and his disciples had also been invited to the wedding. ³ When the wine was gone, Jesus' mother said to him, "They have no more wine." ⁴ "Woman, why do you involve me?" Jesus replied. "My hour has not yet come. ⁵ His mother said to the servants, "Do whatever he tells you." John 2:1-5 (NIV)*

Question 1: What issue arose during the wedding?
- ☐ They ran out of wedding cake.
- ☐ They ran out of seats for their guests.
- ☐ They ran out of wine.

In Jesus' day, weddings were significant events that were long and drawn out -

there was a time of betrothal, a price was paid for the bride, and the wedding feast alone could go on for a week. And it was at such a wedding feast where Jesus was a guest when this humiliating problem arose, the wedding couple ran out of wine. To us, this would be a small thing, but, at that time and place, such an incident would have brought life-long shame to the couple. And this is why Mary turned to Jesus for help. She wanted to spare this couple the shame of their failure.

Jesus responds to His mother in what seems to be an abrupt way by saying, *"My hour has not yet come."* But looking back, we understand that Mary was actually asking no small thing. Where Mary saw the shame of this one moment, Jesus saw the weight of shame and guilt that He would bear for the failures of the whole world. Where Mary was asking Jesus to save one wedding feast, Jesus came to save His bride, and to enjoy an eternal wedding feast with her.

> **Question 2:** In light of John 12:23-32, what was Jesus referring to when He said, "My hour has not yet come"?
> ☐ He was talking about leaving the wedding early.
> ☐ He was talking about the hour He would go to the cross.
> ☐ He was talking about where to find wine.

Jesus was always focused on His primary mission - the work of redemption that He would do on the cross. We know this because throughout His ministry He repeatedly references His upcoming death (Matthew 16:21, Matthew 20:18-19, Matthew 26:1-2).

> *"Nearby stood six stone water jars, the kind used by the Jews for ceremonial washing, each holding from twenty to thirty gallons.* [7] *Jesus said to the servants, "Fill the jars with water"; so they filled them to the brim.* [8] *Then he told them, "Now draw some out and take it to the master of the banquet." John 2:6-8 (NIV)*

> **Question 3:** What was the original use of the water jars?
> ☐ For weddings only.
> ☐ For ceremonial washing.
> ☐ For drinking.

Question 4: How much water did they put into the "empty" jars?
- ☐ They filled them halfway.
- ☐ They filled them two-thirds of the way.
- ☐ They filled them to the brim.

The stone jars were used by the Jews as part of their purification ceremonies under the Old Testament law (Leviticus 15:11, Numbers 8:7). Jesus intentionally chose those jars and instructed the servants to fill them "to the brim" with water. Jesus then transformed the water into wine and sent the servants with the new wine to the "master of the banquet."

> *"and the master of the banquet tasted the water that had been turned into wine. He did not realize where it had come from, though the servants who had drawn the water knew. Then he called the bridegroom aside and said, "Everyone brings out the choice wine first and then the cheaper wine after the guests have had too much to drink, but you have saved the best till now."* [11] *What Jesus did here in Cana of Galilee was the first of the signs through which he revealed his glory, and his disciples believed in him." John 2:9-11 (NIV)*

Remember, this was the first sign of His Messiahship that the disciples witnessed.

Question 5: What were the results of Jesus "revealing His glory"?
- ☐ His disciples could not believe it.
- ☐ His disciples left Him.
- ☐ His disciples believed in Him.

Truly this wedding in Cana was a momentous occasion for many people (the couple, the disciples, Jesus), but its primary significance is that Jesus began to reveal His glory at this wedding. At this wedding, there were hints and indications of the purpose and plan of Jesus' ministry.

Jesus rescued the wedding couple from their failure to provide adequate wine for their guests. By this, He indicated that He was on a mission of rescue to save us from failure and shame. Jesus lived a perfect life and then died the death we deserved to give us His righteousness.

Just as the wedding couple enjoyed the compliments of the Master of Ceremonies for something that Jesus did, we enjoy eternal life and acceptance because of Christ's perfect life attributed to us and His atoning death on the cross in our place. Jesus did the miraculous, transforming work, the wedding couple got the credit for it, *"you have saved the best 'til now."*

Jesus repurposed the stone jars that were for ceremonial washing. By this, He indicated that He would be the One who would cleanse us by washing us with His own blood (1 John 1:7, Revelation 7:14). He was initiating a new covenant with His people sealed with His body broken for us and His blood shed for us.

Jesus did the work of transforming water into wine, which brought joy to the wedding feast. By this, He indicated that He came to do a work of transformation in us (2 Corinthians 5:17) and that He would fill us with inexpressible and glorious joy (Isaiah 25:6, Zechariah 9:16, 1 Peter 1:8 NIV). Jesus would drink the cup of death so that we could drink the cup of joy!

Jesus had the miraculous new wine presented to the master of ceremonies who declared it to be the best wine. After Jesus' death and resurrection, He presented His blood to His Father, who gladly accepted it and declared it to be perfect atoning blood. Jesus' blood is miraculous, transforming us into Jesus' image, making us who were formerly dead and defiled in sin now to be a living and *"a radiant church, without stain or wrinkle or any other blemish, but holy and blameless" (Ephesians 5:27).*

Just as this wedding couple came up short in providing the necessary wine for their wedding feast so too the sacrifices and ceremonies of the Jews could never bring the eternal forgiveness of sins and lasting joy in the heart we all want and need. Hebrews 9:9-10 explains that the system of worship Israel followed was, "an illustration for the present time, indicating that the gifts and sacrifices being offered were not able to clear the conscience of the worshiper. They are only a matter of food and drink and various ceremonial washings— external regulations applying until the time of the new order."

Oh, friend, pause and consider! At the cross, Jesus gave up His life to make us eternally clean. He emptied Himself to *"fill us to the brim."* Through the sacrifice of His own body, He has made us blameless and free from accusation before the Father (Colossians 1:22). And, at His cross, we are being transformed and prepared to be His eternal bride. *"And we all, with unveiled faces, beholding the glory of the Lord, are being transformed into the same image from one degree of glory to another" (2 Corinthians 3:18).*

Just as Jesus saved the wedding feast and provided wine to those in attendance at the marriage in Cana, He has saved us for our eternal wedding to Him and given us the cup of the New Covenant, which is salvation, sanctification, and freedom through His blood, shed on the cross.

> *"And he took bread, gave thanks and broke it, and gave it to them, saying, "This is my body given for you; do this in remembrance of me." [20] In the same way, after the supper he took the cup, saying, "This cup is the new covenant in my blood, which is poured out for you." Luke 22:19-20 (NIV)*

Jesus' body was broken on the cross for us, and in *"breaking the bread"* during communion, we remember that this was His *"body given for you..."* and in *"drinking the cup"* His blood *"...is the new covenant poured out for you."* While Jesus was under the judgment and condemnation of sin, He was crushed under sin's weight and penalty. His body torn to pieces and pressed down to death on the cross. His blood trampled under the feet of those *"who tread in the winepress"* (Isaiah 63:2), *"this cup is the new covenant in my blood."*

Question 6: What are we to remember when Jesus states, "do this in remembrance of me"?
- ☐ That Jesus was a good man and teacher.
- ☐ That Jesus was a good carpenter and craftsman.
- ☐ That Jesus' body was given for you and His blood was poured out for you.

Jesus poured out His life's blood on the cross, and then poured His love and joy into our hearts through the Spirit, *"...God's love has been poured out into our hearts through the Holy Spirit, who has been given to us" (Romans 5:5 NIV).* And in this way, He transforms us from the inside out. We are no longer those who look at what is seen, but instead, we fix our eyes on Jesus, drink the cup of the New Covenant, and experience the love, comfort, and joy of Jesus in all circumstances. (2 Corinthians 4:18)

> *"wine that gladdens human hearts, oil to make their faces shine,*
> *and bread that sustains their hearts." Psalm 104:15 (NIV)*

When we drink of the cup of the New Covenant, our hearts are greatly gladdened and relieved, making our faces shine with joy. As we feast on the bread that is Jesus' broken body, our hearts are sustained and strengthened by grace.

> *"Do not get drunk on wine, which leads to debauchery. Instead,*
> *be filled with the Spirit," Ephesians 5:18 (NIV)*

Believers are not those who turn to alcohol, overeating, sex, media, etc. to intoxicate and fill us; rather, we are filled with the Spirit.

> *"...the fruit of the Spirit is love, joy, peace, forbearance, kindness,*
> *goodness, faithfulness, gentlenesses, and self-control..." Galatians*
> *5:22-23 (NIV)*

As we drink of the cup of the New Covenant, the blood of forgiveness and reconciliation, we are filled with the Spirit, and it will be evident as we bear the fruit of the Spirit. We don't have to try to be loving and kind, but rather, as we abide in Christ, looking always at the cross, we will bear the fruits of His Spirit. The Spirit of God supernaturally produces love, joy, peace, patience, goodness, kindness, and self-control in us.

Jesus' transforming water into wine at the wedding in Cana was a sign pointing to the cross where Jesus would "reveal His glory" to the fullest through His death and resurrection. As His bride, the church, we want to behold Jesus' glory revealed on the cross and help others to see it as well.

When we lift up Jesus and *"reveal His glory"* at the cross, some will have their hearts cut to the core and then healed by Jesus' wounds (1 Peter 2:24). They will be filled to the brim and overflowing with the love and joy of Jesus.

SETTING CAPTIVES FREE

And as they continue to behold the Lord and His glory, their lives will be transformed from the inside out.

> **Question 7:** As you look to the cross and behold the glory of God fully revealed, what do you see? Please share your thoughts.

Friend, do you eagerly anticipate the day when you will see your Bridegroom face to face at the Marriage Supper of the Lamb? Are your eyes and your thoughts fixed on Jesus (Hebrews 3:1, Hebrews 12:1-3) and His glory revealed on the cross? Are you experiencing the heart-filling, life-transforming, joy producing love of God poured out through the Holy Spirit (Romans 5:5) who has been given to you to comfort, counsel, and reveal to you the glories of your eternal Bridegroom? Are you calling others to come and behold the Lamb of God who takes away their sin?

(Revelation 22:17; John 1:29) I hope and pray that you are.

> **Question 8:** How does remembering the death of Jesus, His blood poured out for you on the cross (the wine of the new covenant) and His body broken for you (the bread of the new covenant), help you to prepare for your eternal wedding? Please share.

Christ the Chief Cup— Bearer for the Church

Greetings friend! Today, my hope is that The Church will rediscover The Power of The Cross before going into the world and preaching it to "every creature." The message we teach in Sunday school and preach from the pulpits changes hearts, forgives sins, raises the dead, gives life and puts God's Spirit in whomever believes. The gospel is the only message we have for the church, hidden in the passages of the Old Testament but revealed in Jesus Christ.

In Genesis 37, 39, and 40, we can read about a young man named Joseph, who was betrayed and sold into slavery by his brothers. While working as a slave, Joseph suffered another betrayal, this time by his master's wife, who falsely accused Joseph of raping her. Joseph was innocent of the crime but imprisoned nonetheless. While in prison, Joseph met two prisoners - the Pharaoh's baker and the Pharaoh's cup-bearer.

According to Genesis 40, the Pharaoh's chief cup-bearer and the chief baker offended their royal master and were thrown into prison.

"Pharaoh became angry with these two officials, and he put them in the prison where Joseph was, in the palace of the captain of the guard" (Genesis 40:2-3).

> "While they were in prison, Pharaoh's cup-bearer and baker each had a dream one night, and each dream had its own meaning."
> Genesis 40:5 (NLT)

> "So the chief cup-bearer told Joseph his dream first. "In my dream," he said, "I saw a grapevine in front of me. 10 The vine had three

branches that began to bud and blossom, and soon it produced clusters of ripe grapes. 11 I was holding Pharaoh's wine cup in my hand, so I took a cluster of grapes and squeezed the juice into the cup. Then I placed the cup in Pharaoh's hand." Genesis 40:9-11 (NLT)

Question 1: What did the chief cup-bearer see in front of him?
- ☐ A long life sentence.
- ☐ A grapevine.
- ☐ A way of escape.

Question 2: How many branches did the grapevine have?
- ☐ Twelve branches.
- ☐ Seven branches.
- ☐ Three branches.

"I was holding Pharaoh's wine cup in my hand, so I took a cluster of grapes and squeezed the juice into the cup. Then I placed the cup in Pharaoh's hand" (Genesis 40:11 NLT)

Question 3: Please fill in the blanks. "I was holding Pharaoh's _____ _____ in my hand, so I took a cluster of grapes and _____ the juice into the _____. Then I placed the cup in Pharaoh's hand." (Genesis 40:11 NLT).

I'm sure the chief cup-bearer was desperate to hear "good news" about his dream and a favorable interpretation. In prison, not knowing his outcome, whether he would be given a life sentence, a death sentence or be released from prison and restored to his position.

"This is what the dream means," Joseph said. "The three branches represent three days. Within three days, Pharaoh will lift you up and restore you to your position as his chief cup-bearer." Genesis 40:12-13 (NLT)

Awe yes! After three days, the chief cup-bearer would be lifted up and restored to his position. Can you imagine this? This would be "good news" for anyone put in prison and fearful of the outcome. His life was filled with uncertainty and yet good news came to him that he would be released from prison on the third day, lifted up, restored to his position and would once again serve his royal master and be pardoned from all wrongdoing.

> **Question 4:** According to the interpretation of the dream, what would happen to the chief cup-bearer?
> ☐ After three days, he would have to serve three more years in prison.
> ☐ After three days, he would be lifted up and put to death.
> ☐ After three days, he would be released from prison, lifted up and restored to his position.

Why is this story interjected here when the focus is on Joseph's life journey having been sold into slavery by his brothers? We know every story in God's Word has meaning and each smaller story in the Bible points forward in some way to the main story of the Bible of Jesus' death and resurrection for the church.

And here we learn once again that this story points to Jesus. He is our "Chief Cupbearer." "The Vine," who would grow, bud, be lifted up on the cross and die for us. But after three days be raised to life and restored to His Father. Jesus would drink the cup of His Father's wrath which He willingly took from His hand, *"Take from my hand this cup filled with the wine of my wrath..." So I took the cup from the Lord's hand..." (Jeremiah 25:15;17).*

Friend, Jesus is the Chief Cupbearer who drank every last drop of God's suffering and wrath that was poured out on Him while on the cross. Look with me now at the grapevine in front of you who was squeezed to death and drank the cup for us as He gave up His life to purchase the Church.

Jesus our Chief Cupbearer:

- The cup of suffering
- The cup of the New Covenant
- The cup of bitterness

- The cup that cannot be removed
- The cup we share
- The cup I will not drink again until...

THE CUP OF SUFFERING

> *"He went on a little farther and bowed with his face to the ground, praying, "My Father! If it is possible, let this cup of suffering be taken away from me. Yet I want your will to be done, not mine." Matthew 26:39 (NLT)*

Jesus drank the cup of suffering for you and in your place and mine as He went to the cross. He suffered far greater than any human has ever suffered because He was bearing the sins of the world as He drank this cup of suffering. Jesus drank the cup of suffering so you could drink the cup of blessing and forgiveness.

THE CUP OF THE NEW COVENANT

> *"And he took a cup of wine and gave thanks to God for it. He gave it to them and said, "Each of you drink from it, 28 for this is my blood, which confirms the covenant between God and his people. It is poured out as a sacrifice to forgive the sins of many." Matthew 26:27-28 (NLT)*

Jesus poured out this cup of the New Covenant for you. It was in pouring out His blood as a sin offering on the altar of the cross where the curtain was torn, providing access to God the Father. The New Covenant was instituted through the tearing of the curtain, the tearing of Jesus' flesh so that by His wounds, you could be both healed and forgiven (Hebrews 10:20). Jesus fulfilled the Old Covenant in our place, keeping the Law perfectly for us, and at His death, He instituted a New Covenant based on forgiveness of sin.

THE CUP OF BITTERNESS

> *"But Jesus answered by saying to them, "You don't know what you are asking! Are you able to drink from the bitter cup of suffering I am about to drink?" "Oh yes," they replied, "we are able!" Matthew 20:22 (NLT)*

Jesus drank down the bitter cup of suffering so that all our bitterness may come to a complete end through His death. He took the bitter cup from you and drank it for you. He drank down this cup so that your cup might be sweet. Jesus is The Vine that was squeezed into the cup, who drank our bitter cup "for us," which in turn satisfies our souls and removes our bitterness "from us." (Exodus 15:22-25)

THE CUP THAT CANNOT BE REMOVED

> *"Then Jesus left them a second time and prayed, "My Father! If this cup cannot be taken away unless I drink it, your will be done." Matthew 26:42 (NLT)*

Friend, unless Jesus drinks this cup, sin cannot be removed from us. In other words, if Jesus did not drink the cup of suffering and wrath, God's wrath could not be removed from us as we would still be under sin's judgment and penalty. We find our life in Jesus' suffering and death because He indeed did drink the cup. And because He drank the cup, God's wrath has been taken away from us. This was the Father's will that He would send His Son to drink the cup to be our propitiation (Romans 3:25).

> *"God sent him to die in our place to take away our sins. We receive forgiveness through faith in the blood of Jesus' death. This showed that God always does what is right and fair, as in the past, when he was patient and did not punish people for their sins." Romans 3:25 (NCV)*

THE CUP WE SHARE

"Is not the cup of thanksgiving for which we give thanks a participation in the blood of Christ? And is not the bread that we break a participation in the body of Christ?" 1 Corinthians 10:16 (NIV)

Jesus drank the cup of death so that we could drink the cup of life! Jesus drank the cup of judgment so that we can drink the cup of forgiveness! Jesus drank the cup of condemnation so that we could drink the cup of salvation and sanctification! Jesus drank the cup of God's wrath, but we drink the cup of thanksgiving! At the cross, we have "participated" in the death of Christ and, therefore, also the resurrection of Christ as we have taken of the bread that was broken for us and the cup that was poured out for us. *"For you died, and your life is now hidden with Christ in God" (Colossians 3:3 NIV).*

Question 5: What thoughts do you have about this "cup of thanksgiving" and the "bread we break" as you consider the cross and what Jesus did for you?

- A grapevine in front of me
- The vine had three branches
- It began to bud and blossom
- It produced clusters of ripe grapes
- I was holding Pharaoh's wine cup in my hand
- I took a cluster of grapes and squeezed the juice into the cup
- I placed the cup in Pharaoh's hand

Jesus is The Grapevine in front of you with the three branches *"that began to bud and blossom, and soon it produced clusters of ripe grapes."* In the prime of His life and ministry, Jesus' life would be cut short as He would go to the cross and hang like grapes hanging from their vines. *"So, I took a cluster of grapes and squeezed the juice into the cup."* Can you see Him now, that this Grapevine that budded in the prime of His life was squeezed and crushed in the winepress of God's wrath then poured out like wine for you?

> *"I have trodden the winepress alone, and from the peoples no one was with me; I trod them in my anger and trampled them in my wrath; their lifeblood spattered on my garments, and stained all my apparel." (Isaiah 63:3)*

Oh, friend, Jesus would go to the cross, be imprisoned there, nailed to a tree like a criminal so we could be set free like the chief cup-bearer who was released from prison and restored to his position on the third day. Jesus would rise from the dead on the third day, restore us to the Father through His shed blood, as He was restored to the right hand of the Father. Now pleading on our behalf with His wounds. The same wounds used to heal and cleanse you are the same wounds that keep and protect you.

The Cup I will not drink again until…

> *"Mark my words—I will not drink wine again until the day I drink it new with you in my Father's Kingdom." ³⁰Then they sang a hymn and went out to the Mount of Olives." Matthew 26:29-30 (NLT)*

Here Jesus connects His death with the culmination of all things with the marriage supper of the Lamb. In communion, we look back, and our hearts hurt to see the suffering of Christ on the cross in our place, but we also look forward, and our hearts are made whole at the contemplation of our being with our Bridegroom face to face. He died for us; He rose for us! He is now interceding for us and preparing a place for us. And one glorious day, we will gather with Him to drink the cup with Him.

Question 6: Please provide your final thoughts and comments about today's lesson, what you learned or remembered:

_____

_____

_____

_____

Christ the Chief Baker for the Church

*I*n our last lesson, we looked at "Christ The Chief Cup-Bearer for the Church." Today, we'll see how Christ is also The Chief Baker for the Church.

By way of review we remember, while Joseph was in prison he met two prisoners - the Pharaoh's baker and the Pharaoh's cup-bearer. And according to Genesis 40, the Pharaoh's chief cup-bearer and the chief baker offended their royal master and were thrown into prison.

> *"Pharaoh became angry with these two officials, and he put them in the prison where Joseph was, in the palace of the captain of the guard." Genesis 40:2-3*

> *"While they were in prison, Pharaoh's cup-bearer and baker each had a dream one night, and each dream had its own meaning." Genesis 40:5 (NLT)*

Joseph gave his first interpretation to the chief cup-bearer which was a very positive interpretation of his dream, especially for one imprisoned and with an unknown future. Now it is the chief baker's turn to share and hear his interpretation of the dream he had. I'm sure he was hopeful that he would receive the same favorable interpretation of his dream the chief cup-bearer heard of his.

> *"When the chief baker saw that Joseph had given the first dream such a positive interpretation, he said to Joseph, "I had a dream, too. In my dream, there were three baskets of white pastries stacked on my head. [17] The top basket contained all kinds of*

pastries for Pharaoh, but the birds came and ate them from the basket on my head." Genesis 40:16-17 (NLT)

Question 1: What was inside the baskets on the chief baker's head?
- ☐ Bread
- ☐ Stones
- ☐ Barley

Question 2: How many baskets of bread were on the chief baker's head?
- ☐ One
- ☐ Two
- ☐ Three

"This is what the dream means," Joseph told him. "The three baskets also represent three days. ¹⁹ Three days from now Pharaoh will lift you up and impale your body on a pole. Then birds will come and peck away at your flesh." Genesis 40:18-19 (NLT)

Question 3: Please fill in the blanks. "Three days from now Pharaoh will _____ _____ _____ and _____ your _____ on a _____. Then birds will come and peck away at your flesh." Genesis 40:19 (NLT)

I can't imagine hearing the interpretation of this dream! Oh, what a shock it must have been. How agonizing it would be waiting three more days to see if the interpretation of the dreams would prove to be true. One man was excited to be lifted up and restored to his original position and the other terribly frightened that he would be lifted up to and put to death on a pole.

As we take a look at this dream we can see how it shows the wonder, beauty and joy of the cross.

Pastries (bread) in the baskets: The chief baker had bread in the baskets on top of his head. Evil men took "The Bread of life", struck His flesh and tore it apart like the birds that ate the bread out of the baskets, beating Jesus within an inch of His life and hanging Him on a pole (Numbers 21:9; John 3:14).

"So Jesus said again, "I tell you the truth, unless you eat the flesh of the Son of Man and drink his blood, you cannot have eternal life within you." John 6:53 NLT

"Jesus said, "I tell you the truth, Moses didn't give you bread from heaven. My Father did. And now he offers you the true bread from heaven. 33 The true bread of God is the one who comes down from heaven and gives life to the world." John 6:32-33 NLT

"For it is my Father's will that all who see his Son and believe in him should have eternal life. I will raise them up at the last day." John 6:40 NLT

Oh friend, do you see Jesus being lifted up for you. Dying on the pole for you. Breathing His last breath and giving up His spirit so you could receive the Spirit of life, love, and liberty! Come and see and partake of the bread broken for you! Come and die to self and sin and be raised now to new life walking in the power of the Spirit!

Baskets on top of the chief baker's head: The chief baker had three baskets full of bread on top of his head in his dream. The baskets would have been made from twigs woven together to hold the bread. Jesus had a crown of thorns woven together and pressed into His head. Not a crown of honor but a crown of dishonor and disgrace that pierced His head, wearing and carrying the curse of sin and death, thorns and thistles in His flesh.

"...the ground is cursed because of you. All your life you will struggle to scratch a living from it. 18 It will grow thorns and thistles for you..." Genesis 3:17-18 NLT

"Then Pilate had Jesus flogged with a lead-tipped whip. ² The soldiers wove a crown of thorns and put it on his head, and they put a purple robe on him. ³ "Hail! King of the Jews!" they mocked, as they slapped him across the face." John 19:1-3 NLT

Under the immediate sentence of death: The chief baker was under the sentence of death upon hearing the interpretation of the dream but it would not be carried out until the third day. Jesus was under the constant sentence of death but it wouldn't be carried out for thirty-three years.

> *"After the wise men were gone, an angel of the Lord appeared to Joseph in a dream. "Get up! Flee to Egypt with the child and his mother," the angel said. "Stay there until I tell you to return, because Herod is going to search for the child to kill him." Matthew 2:13 NLT*

Jesus entered our death sentence while on the cross, (He took the "sticks of death" from us) was hungry and thirsty as He tasted death for us so we could live through Him (Hebrews 2:9).

> *"And Christ lives within you, so even though your body will die because of sin, the Spirit gives you life because you have been made right with God." Romans 8:10 NLT*

> *"But Christ has rescued us from the curse pronounced by the law. When he was hung on the cross, he took upon himself the curse for our wrongdoing. For it is written in the Scriptures, "Cursed is everyone who is hung on a tree." Galatians 3:13 NLT*

The same day the chief baker was lifted up on the pole and put to death, the chief cup-bearer was lifted up and restored: The chief cup-bearer and the chief baker were thrown into prison for their wrongdoing, for upsetting and making Pharaoh angry enough to put them in prison. Both were sentenced on the same day—one was hung on a pole and the other restored to his position. Jesus fulfilled both The Chief Baker who was lifted up and impaled on the pole and the Chief Cup-Bearer who was lifted up out of the prison and restored to his previous position on the third day.

And now think about the application of this passage to your own heart and life. Friend, the same day of your physical birth you were sentenced to death (Psalm 51:5), but the same day you believed the message of the cross is the same day you died with Christ, your flesh was cut away, your sins were forgiven and you rose from the dead and seated with Christ in heaven! The same day you died with Christ you rose in Christ!

> *"But God is so rich in mercy, and he loved us so much, [5] that even though we were dead because of our sins, he gave us life when he raised Christ from the dead. (It is only by God's grace that you have been saved!) [6] For he raised us from the dead along with Christ and seated us with him in the heavenly realms because we are united with Christ Jesus." Ephesians 2:4-6 NLT*

> *"You were dead because of your sins and because your sinful nature was not yet cut away. Then God made you alive with Christ, for he forgave all our sins." Colossians 2:13 NLT*

The baker and cup-bearer would taste the food and drink from the cup to ensure that the Pharaoh would not be poisoned to death. But, "Jesus tasted death for everyone" (Hebrews 2:9) with His sacrifice on the cross, our anointed bread in the basket (Leviticus 8:31), the living bread that was burned up in the fire of God's wrath (Leviticus 8:32).

> *"I am the living bread that came down from heaven. Anyone who eats this bread will live forever; and this bread, which I will offer so the world may live, is my flesh." John 6:51 NLT*

> **Question 4:** Please fill in the blanks. "I am the _____ _____ that came down from heaven. Anyone who eats this _____ will live forever; and this _____ which I will offer so the world may live, is my _____." John 6:51

The real bread from heaven is Jesus' flesh which He would offer to the world. Jesus, the bread of life would go to the cross and be baked in the oven of God's wrath. With the leaven of our sin so He could rise from the dead and give Himself to all who come, see and believe.

"Jesus replied, "I am the bread of life. Whoever comes to me will never be hungry again. Whoever believes in me will never be thirsty." John 6:35 NLT

Friend, Jesus is the "white" bread that came down from heaven (Genesis 40:16 NLT). The One who was dressed in scarlet and made red like crimson bleeding from head to toe while on the cross to make you white as snow (Isaiah 1:18). Jesus unclothed Himself of His majesty and honor to take the place of dishonor and humility, clothing Himself with human flesh sin and death to save and sanctify you. Now pleading with His wounds for you to come and see. Come and believe. Come to Jesus and receive the cup of wine and the bread broken in pieces for you.

"For I pass on to you what I received from the Lord himself. On the night when he was betrayed, the Lord Jesus took some bread ²⁴and gave thanks to God for it. Then he broke it in pieces and said, "This is my body, which is given for you. Do this in remembrance of me." ²⁵In the same way, he took the cup of wine after supper, saying, "This cup is the new covenant between God and his people—an agreement confirmed with my blood. Do this in remembrance of me as often as you drink it." ²⁶For every time you eat this bread and drink this cup, you are announcing the Lord's death until he comes again." 1 Corinthians 11:23-26

Question 5: What thoughts do you have of Jesus now as you look at The Bead of Life broken in pieces for you?

_____

_____

_____

Dear, pastor, elder, church leader or member, what a privilege and honor we have to share the cup and the bread together. We are to always remember the cross. Remember the price paid. Remember the suffering servant. Remember that there is power only in the blood of Christ. Power that removes sin from us and power to keep us from being removed out of His hand! Of friend, let's pray together that the church rediscovers the power of Jesus' death and resurrection and becomes immovable from it!

The Cross Makes Us New Creations

*D*ear friend, welcome back! What a blessing it is to look to Jesus together with you.

We know that the gospel, Jesus' death for the forgiveness of sins, His burial, and His rising from the dead on the third day is of first importance as outlined in (1 Corinthians 15:3-4), the reason this course exists. We also know the gospel was God's plan before the foundation of the world (Ephesians 1:4). Because of this, we should be able to see the gospel from Genesis 1:1 to Revelation 22:21. So, let's begin our study today beginning with Genesis chapter 1.

> *"In the beginning, God created the heavens and the earth. [2] The earth was without form and void, and darkness was over the face of the deep. And the Spirit of God was hovering over the face of the waters. [3] And God said, "Let there be light," and there was light. [4] And God saw that the light was good. And God separated the light from the darkness. [5] God called the light Day, and the darkness he called Night. And there was evening and there was morning, the first day." Genesis 1:1-5*

Question 1: How has Genesis 1:2 characterized your life prior to knowing Christ? Please share your thoughts.

_____

_____

_____

Our lives were just like the earth, in fact, we could say, "In the beginning" our lives were without form and in an uninhabitable state, void and buried in the darkness of the deep. The word translated as "deep" here means a "great abyss" or deepest darkest waters. But thankfully, God's plan prior to the foundation of the world was to save the world by sending His Son, not to condemn the world but that the world might be saved through Him (John 3:17).

"And God said, "Let there be light," and there was light" Genesis 1:3

Question 2: How does Genesis 1:3 point us to the cross of Christ, The Light of the world who would take away our sin?
- ☐ God shone light into the darkness of the world, but it didn't help.
- ☐ God shone The Light of Christ: His life, death, burial, and resurrection, into the darkness of the world.
- ☐ God shone the light into the darkness of the world.

Yes, when God said, "let there be light" everything changed and the uninhabitable became habitable, took on form, was no longer void or empty and darkness was separated from the light. And this light that God saw as "good" became Good News to us! *"The people who walked in darkness have seen a great light; those who dwelt in a land of deep darkness, on them has light shone"* (Isaiah 9:2).

"And God saw that the light was good. And God separated the light from the darkness." Genesis 1:4

Question 3: Please fill in the blanks. "And God saw that the _____ was _____. And God separated the _____ from the _____." Genesis 1:4.

Before Christ rescued us out of the darkness we walked in the darkness. Some for many years which made our lives seem worthless, formless, powerless, and void of anything good. But at the cross, God lifted us out of this darkness, by sending His own Son in the likeness of sinful flesh, to be a sin offering for us (Romans 8:3).

"for at one time you were darkness, but now you are light in the Lord. Walk as children of light" Ephesians 5:8

"For God has done what the law, weakened by the flesh, could not do. By sending his own Son in the likeness of sinful flesh and for sin, he condemned sin in the flesh," Romans 8:3

At the cross, we are crucified with Christ, and raised with Christ in His resurrection. And by His Spirit living with us Christ is formed in us, "my little children, for whom I am again in the anguish of childbirth until Christ is formed in you!" (Galatians 4:19). Those who believe this message of power and love no longer are void, but instead are filled with Christ, having Christ formed in them and in this powerful cross where Jesus died we see *"light shining out of darkness."*

When we preach or teach Jesus Christ and him crucified, we call our listeners attention to the cross where they will see, Jesus, who carried their sorrows, was stricken, smitten by God, afflicted, left for dead, separated from His Father, hanging on the cross without form, void and empty of human or heavenly help. This is the place where His blood poured out like water, nailed to the tree to die in the darkness of death (Psalm 22:14). Then Jesus went even deeper into the darkness, the grave, and into "the heart of the earth" (Matthew 12:40). He lay there for three days, so He could go down to the depths of death for us and raise us up from the dead with Him.

> **Question 4:** Are you beginning to see, or have you seen the gospel emerging from Genesis 1?
> ☐ Yes, I am.
> ☐ Maybe a little.
> ☐ No, not at all.

"God called the light Day, and the darkness he called Night. And there was evening and there was morning, the first day." Genesis 1:5

Question 5: On what day did all that we've studied so far take place?

☐ On the seventh day.

☐ On the thirteenth day.

☐ On the first day.

Yes, this all happened on the "first day" of creation. God showing and teaching us the light of the gospel that shined out of the darkness and into our hearts is truly of "first importance." The very first chapter of the Bible shows the work of the cross where God makes us "new creations" purchased with the blood of Christ. His death on the cross and resurrection from the dead. The cross makes the uninhabitable habitable (the Holy Spirit comes to live in us), separates light from darkness, raises us out of the deepest darkness, forms us into the image of Christ and fills our empty lives completely to the brim!

"For God, who said, "Let light shine out of darkness," has shone in our hearts to give the light of the knowledge of the glory of God in the face of Jesus Christ." 2 Corinthians 4:6

Question 6: Please fill in the blanks. "For God, who said, "Let light shine out of darkness," has shone in our _____ to give the _____ of the _____ of the _____ of _____ in the _____ of _____ _____" (2 Corinthians 4:6).

"And God said, "Let the waters under the heavens be gathered together into one place, and let the dry land appear." And it was so. [10] God called the dry land Earth, and the waters that were gathered together he called Seas. And God saw that it was good. [11] And God said, "Let the earth sprout vegetation, plants yielding seed, and fruit trees bearing fruit in which is their seed, each according to its kind, on the earth." And it was so. [12] The earth brought forth vegetation, plants yielding seed according to their own kinds, and trees bearing fruit in which is their seed, each according to its kind. And God saw that it was good. [13] And there

was evening and there was morning, the third day." Genesis 1:9-13

We first noticed that in the beginning, the earth was without form, void and in darkness, which characterizes our lives living in the darkness, or as the Bible describes us as being "dead in sin and trespass" (Ephesians 2:1) prior to knowing Christ and experiencing the power of the cross.

Now we're going to look further into God's incredible Word to see how creation continues to reveal the gospel and the growth of the believer's life through Jesus' death and resurrection.

> *"And God said, "Let the waters under the heavens be gathered together into one place, and let the dry land appear." And it was so." Genesis 1:9*

Question 7: What significant event took place here in Genesis 1:9?
- ☐ The waters are still there waiting for God's next command.
- ☐ The waters were gathered into one place and dry ground appeared.
- ☐ The waters flowed into many places and the wet ground disappeared.

Friend, here we have the rising of the dry ground coming up from the deep dark place where it was once void and without form. This is very much like our lives when the light shone into the darkness of our lives with the "good news" of Jesus' death and resurrection. The Light shone into our dark hearts and lifted us up and out of the darkness. It didn't just lift us up out of the darkness but set our feet firmly on solid "dry ground" just like it did with the Israelites when they "saw" the "salvation of the Lord" and walked through the Red Sea on dry ground, out of the land of slavery, and where their enemy was defeated (Exodus 14:16-29).

> *"God called the dry land Earth, and the waters that were gathered together he called Seas. And God saw that it was good. 11 And God said, "Let the earth sprout vegetation, plants yielding seed,*

and fruit trees bearing fruit in which is their seed, each according to its kind, on the earth." And it was so." Genesis 1:10-11

Question 8: What happened to the dry ground once it was raised from the deep?
- ☐ The earth sprouted fruitless evergreens, plants yielding without seed, and fruit trees that bore no fruit.
- ☐ The earth sprouted thorns, plants yielding thorns, and fruit trees bearing no fruit.
- ☐ The earth sprouted vegetation, plants yielding seed, and fruit trees bearing fruit in which is their seed.

"The earth brought forth vegetation, plants yielding seed according to their own kinds, and trees bearing fruit in which is their seed, each according to its kind. And God saw that it was good. [13] And there was evening and there was morning, the third day." Genesis 1:12-13

Question 9: What day did dry ground, vegetation, plants yielding seed, and trees bearing fruit appear?
- ☐ On the first day.
- ☐ On the second day.
- ☐ On the third day.

The Light of Jesus Christ shines into the darkness, we believe and receive the message of the cross by faith and God separates us from the darkness. We were once dead and without hope, then we rose to live new lives through the powerful working of God and we share in the resurrection of Jesus Christ. Look at the stages of "growth" all believers can experience as we hear the message of the cross from the pulpit of churches and walk by the Spirit we grow and mature in Christ begin bearing fruit for His glory.

"...having been buried with him in baptism, in which you were also raised with him through faith in the powerful working of God, who raised him from the dead." Colossians 2:12

Notice the growth that raised up on the third day:

- Sprout vegetation
- Plants yielding seed
- Fruit trees bearing fruit in which is their seed

Sprout vegetation: A new believer who has been crucified with Christ, raised with Christ, and is sprouting vegetation as his/her faith is in its infancy, new, but very real. Vegetation spreads but its roots have not matured and its height is not established.

Plants yielding seed: A believer who has been crucified with Christ, raised with Christ, and is moving into maturity like a plant yielding its seeds. Their faith is growing and they have begun scattering the seed of the Word of God.

Fruit trees bearing fruit in which is their seed: A believer who has been crucified with Christ, raised with Christ, and is moving into maturity and building strength with deeper roots like a tree bearing fruit. Because they are rooted at the cross, they are healthy bearing fruit and scattering the seed of the Word of God.

> *"Other seeds fell on good soil and produced grain, some a hundredfold, some sixty, some thirty." Matthew 13:8*

> *"...because of the hope laid up for you in heaven. Of this you have heard before in the word of the truth, the gospel, ⁶ which has come to you, as indeed in the whole world it is bearing fruit and increasing—as it also does among you, since the day you heard it and understood the grace of God in truth, ⁷ just as you learned it from Epaphras our beloved fellow servant. He is a faithful minister of Christ on your behalf" Colossians 1:5-7*

Question 10: If you're a pastor, elder or teacher are you proclaiming the message of the cross as of first importance from the pulpit, bible study, or Sunday school teachings? If you're a church member are you hearing the message of the cross in your church? Finally, can you see how we are to grow and mature to bear more and more fruit when Jesus' death and resurrection are proclaimed? Please share your thoughts.

_____

_____

_____

_____

Brothers and sisters, let's look at the cross, using the perspective of Genesis 1, and rejoice. We were empty (void), in darkness, and buried in the great abyss of sin (waters of darkness).

But then God shone His light into our hearts, by showing us how Jesus Christ came to this world and entered into our condition. On the cross, Jesus entered the deep darkness, taking on your sin and all sickness and sorrows, there He emptied Himself (Philippians 2:7) pouring out His very life unto death for you, and shortly after was buried in the tomb. Yet on the third day, He rose from the dead, and we rose from our sin by His resurrection power, and now we are children of the light who walk in newness of life. We were empty, in darkness and buried in sin, but now have been raised up as new creations in Christ (2 Corinthians 5:17) and are filled with God's Spirit, walking in the light.

Let's rejoice in our own transformation at the cross, and commit to giving out this message of the death of Jesus for our sins and of His resurrection from the dead; the message of transformation and new life!

Having Our Eyes Opened
to see the Gospel

*T*oday, I want to study with you about how Jesus taught us to see His death and resurrection in the Scriptures. We'll also see what has to happen for us to do so.

In Luke 24, we read about two disciples walking on the road to Emmaus when Jesus walked up to them and joined in their conversation. However, something unusual took place when Jesus walked up to them: *"But God kept them from recognizing him" (Luke 24:16).* Wow, that's strange, isn't it? They were looking right at Jesus but didn't recognize Him.

The rest of the story tells us that Jesus asked the two disciples what they were talking about, and they explained that Jesus Christ, the miracle-working prophet and mighty teacher, was condemned to death by the religious leaders and then crucified. These disciples had hoped that Jesus had come to rescue Israel, but instead, He had died on a cross three days ago (Luke 24:19-21).

Then went on to explain how some of their women had gone to the tomb earlier in the morning and "they said his body was missing, and they had seen angels who told them Jesus is alive!" (Luke 24:23). These two disciples were perplexed, confused, and bewildered, not knowing what to believe or what was happening.

Question 1: Can you venture a guess, at this point, as to why these disciples were perplexed and confused about Jesus' death and the reports of His resurrection? What are your thoughts?

_____

_____

_____

Jesus tells us why the disciples were confused and bewildered:

> *"Then Jesus said to them, "You foolish people! You find it so hard to believe all that the prophets wrote in the Scriptures. 26 Wasn't it clearly predicted that the Messiah would have to suffer all these things before entering his glory?" Luke 24:25-26 (NLT)*

Question 2: According to Luke 24:25-26, why should the disciples have been very clear about what had happened to Jesus?

_____

_____

_____

Question 3: What did Jesus say was written in "all the prophets"? Please fill in the blanks: "Wasn't it clearly predicted that the _____ would have to _____ _____ these _____ before entering _____ _____?"

If these disciples had read and believed the Old Testament, they would have understood that Jesus' mission was to suffer and die to rescue Israel and all who believe, from our sins, and to rise from the dead on the third day and enter His glory in heaven.

Indeed, this was THE subject of the Old Testament! It's the main point of the entire Bible, that which is of first importance (1 Corinthians 15:1-6), the primary message of every Book, the message God gave to the church to proclaim from every Book in the Bible!

> *"Then Jesus took them through the writings of Moses and all the prophets, explaining from all the Scriptures the things concerning himself (emphasis mine)." Luke 24:27 (NLT)*

Question 4: According to Luke 24:27, what books of the Old Testament speak of Jesus, His death and resurrection?

_____

_____

_____

_____

Now, these disciples were very familiar with the Old Testament, most had read and even memorized large passages of it. They had looked right at the pages of Scripture but did not recognize Jesus in it. It's almost as if they were kept from recognizing Him in the pages of the Book, like they were blinded to the good news of His death and resurrection.

And, friend, this is the way we are all born! We are blind to the good news of Jesus' suffering in our place, His wounds which heal us, His blood which saves us, His death which frees us. We can be Bible scholars and seminary-trained professionals, and still miss the main message of the Bible as it is shown in every Book of the Old Testament.

What needs to happen for us to begin to see this precious and powerful message?

> *"As they sat down to eat, he took the bread and blessed it. Then he broke it and gave it to them. [31] Suddenly, their eyes were opened, and they recognized him. And at that moment he disappeared!" Luke 24:30-31 (NLT)*

Question 5: What happened to the disciples so that they could finally recognize Jesus?

_____

_____

_____

_____

Friend, a miracle needs to be performed for us to recognize Jesus in the pages of the Bible. We require divine intervention for us to stop misinterpreting Scripture by leaving the suffering and glories of the Messiah out of it. God has to open our eyes, hearts, minds, and understanding so that we can see the glories of Calvary, the wonder of redemption, the beautiful, wonderful, terrible cross, and the mighty resurrection of Jesus (see Acts 16:14).

And this thought brings us back to the beginning of our story, where God kept the disciples from recognizing Jesus as He walked along with them. Why did God do this? What was He teaching those disciples, and us, by keeping them from recognizing Jesus?

It makes sense now. Jesus was giving these disciples an object lesson, a picture story of the truth He just taught them. Just as they were walking along with Jesus and looking right at Him, but didn't recognize Him, even so they were reading their Bibles, looking directly at it, but didn't recognize Jesus in the pages. They didn't see the message of His suffering and death for their sin, His resurrection for their justification, His ascension to glory.

Imagine those disciples talking with each other after this event. This isn't recorded for us in Scripture but we can imagine an exchange similar to the one below. We'll call one disciple Malcolm and the other Clopas:

Malcolm: "Can you believe we were walking right along with Jesus, talking to Him and listening to Him, and we didn't even recognize Him? I mean, we were looking right at His face, looking into His eyes, but not understanding who He was! Wow, we were truly blind, weren't we?"

Clopas: "Yes, we were! But what's even more amazing is that you and I have been reading our Bibles for years, looking right into its pages, and we didn't recognize Jesus in it. For all these years we missed that the Messiah would be beaten and wounded for our transgressions, that He would be bruised for our iniquities (Isaiah 53:5), that He would be struck on the face with a rod (Micah 5:1). We didn't understand that He would be killed and crucified on a tree (Deuteronomy 21:23) and that He would rise from the dead on the third day (Hosea 6:1-2, Jonah 2). Talk about blindness!"

Malcolm: "Yes, and oh how thankful I am that Jesus miraculously opened my eyes, and I finally recognized Him! I mean I really saw it was Him! And now that's how I read my Bible, too! He's opened my eyes to see Him in every book on every page! Yes, I finally understand that Jesus was put into the deep sleep of death and had His side opened so that I might become His bride (Genesis 2). I see that He was my Passover Lamb who saved me from the wrath of God (Exodus 12), and my Scapegoat who bore my sin away (Leviticus 16). I finally see clearly! Just yesterday, I was reading and saw Jesus as the end of the "seventy sevens" who came to "finish transgression", to put an end to my sin, and to bring in everlasting righteousness. Yes, my sin is gone, and I'm righteous through His suffering death and powerful resurrection. Oh, Clopas, I can finally see! My heart is burning with love for Jesus like never before!"

> *"They said to each other, "Didn't our hearts burn within us as he talked with us on the road and explained the Scriptures to us?" Luke 24:32 (NLT)*

Question 6: Please share your thoughts on the above conversation. What did these two disciples learn through this experience?

Oh, friend, once God opens our eyes to the central message of the Bible, the sufferings and glories of the Messiah, we begin to see Him everywhere! With our eyes opened to see Jesus, our hearts burn with love!

We see Him as the Seed of the woman (Genesis 3:15) who would destroy the head of the serpent, the devil himself, but would be bruised in His flesh while doing so. Oh, our hearts do BURN with love for Him as we see Him climbing Calvary's hill, weighed down with a cross and our sins, going there for us to fight Satan. We see Him bruised in His flesh, pierced and wounded there, wearing a crown of thorns and suffering death, all that He would defeat our enemy and secure our victory and freedom. *"In this way, he disarmed the spiritual rulers and authorities. He shamed them publicly by his victory over them on the cross"* (Colossians 2:15).

We see Him nailed to the tree of Calvary, remembering that anyone hung up on a tree is under God's curse (Deuteronomy 21:23), and this good news causes us to rejoice. Seeing Jesus, our hearts overflow with love that He would stoop so low as to receive our curse, take our separation from God, that we might enjoy eternal blessings from our Father, being united with Him forever.

As we keep looking there at Calvary, our hearts keep expanding, bigger and bigger, as God pours out His love into our hearts by His Spirit (Romans 5:5). Looking to Jesus, we become awestruck, our mouths gaping open at the sight of Love crucified for us, and of Forgiveness rising out of the grave for us. Our hearts burn and break, are crushed and cured, are torn and treated, all at the cross of Calvary, all by the resurrection power of the Living Jesus.

> **Question 7:** Do you see how the church needs to rediscover the gospel? Do you understand that this is the one message of power and love? Have your eyes been opened to see the need to focus on THIS message of the dying and rising Messiah? The crucified and risen Christ? Have you made the connection between seeing the cross/resurrection of Jesus and having your heart burn with love for Him? Please make an honest assessment and answer these questions as you feel led:

The Cross Focused Prayer of the Lord

Today, we're going to study a very familiar prayer and passage typically known as, "The Lord's Prayer." Jesus gave this prayer as an example to His disciples which is the base and basic of all prayers. This prayer is not meant to simply be repeated as we read it but rather we are to pray it in remembrance of the cross on which Jesus died. Jesus was teaching His disciples how to pray and therefore this applies to all believers; how we should likewise pray. Jesus is teaching us how to pray with "the power of the cross" that purchased The Church, rescues souls, forgives sins, and makes us part of the body of Christ.

Before Jesus taught how to pray, He first teaches two ways we should not pray.

> *"When you pray, don't be like the hypocrites who love to pray publicly on street corners and in the synagogues where everyone can see them" (Matthew 6:5 NLT).*

> *"When you pray, don't babble on and on as the Gentiles do. They think their prayers are answered merely by repeating their words again and again" (Matthew 6:7 NLT).*

We are not to pray to be seen which would puff us up as if we were some sort of super prayer warriors, nor babble like the Gentiles thinking we will be heard by vain repetition or our many words. No, we bow our knees before the Father who sent His Son to die our death, pay our penalty and rescue us from Satan and sins power. So, we bow in humility on bended knees as we come and let our requests be known.

"Pray like this: Our Father in heaven, may your name be kept holy.
[10]May your Kingdom come soon. May your will be done on earth,
as it is in heaven. [11]Give us today the food we need, [12] and forgive
us our sins, as we have forgiven those who sin against us. [13] And
don't let us yield to temptation, but rescue us from the evil one"
(Matthew 6:9-13 NLT).

Question 1: Jesus is teaching believers how to pray and in this teaching whose Father is in heaven?
- ☐ Our Father.
- ☐ Only a priest can be called Father.
- ☐ Anyone's Father.

All believers are part of the family of God having been adopted, not by a court through the legal process of this world, but by the highest court in heaven—purchased with the blood of Jesus Christ. We are adopted into the body of Christ whereby God became "Our Father". "God decided in advance to adopt us into his own family by bringing us to himself through Jesus Christ. This is what he wanted to do, and it gave him great pleasure" (Ephesians 1:5 NLT).

Our Heavenly Father loved us so much that He adopted us as sons and daughters, through Jesus Christ. And friend, we have been loved by Jesus the same way in which our Father in heaven loves His very own Son. *"I have loved you even as the Father has loved me. Remain in my love"* (John 15:9).

This love of Jesus took Him to the cross, where He was in a sense, disowned by God, forsaken by His Father as the relationship between them was broken because of our sin. Jesus cried out, *"My God, my God, why have you forsaken me?"* (Matthew 27:46), experiencing the abandonment of His Father as Jesus carried our sin and took our judgment.

Notice, Jesus did not use His usual term, "Father" but rather "my God." He was rejected and forsaken by His Father so that you and I could call God "Father" as we enter His family by faith in the finished work of the cross.

"...when the right time came, God sent his Son, born of a woman,
subject to the law.[5] God sent him to buy freedom for us who
were slaves to the law, so that he could adopt us as his very own

children. ⁶ And because we are his children, God has sent the Spirit of his Son into our hearts, prompting us to call out, "Abba, Father." ⁷ Now you are no longer a slave but God's own child. And since you are his child, God has made you his heir." Galatians 4:4-7

The important point is this: we are no longer "slaves" (John 8:35) or "children of wrath" (Ephesians 2:3) or "children of the devil" (John 8:44), but rather children of God and can call God "Father", or call out "Abba, Father." *"See what an incredible quality of love the Father has shown to us, that we would [be permitted to] be named and called and counted the children of God! And so we are!"* (1 John 3:1 AMP)

We can pray "Our Father in heaven" because of the cross!

> *"Pray like this: Our Father in heaven, may your name be kept holy." (Matthew 6:9 NLT)*

The last part of verse 9 says, *"may your name be kept holy."* Only One who was sinless and holy could keep God's name holy (Leviticus 11:44-45) which begs the question: how might God's name be kept holy? What event would take place where God's name would be *"kept holy"*?

God's name kept holy in Christ: *"Now I am departing from the world; they are staying in this world, but I am coming to you. Holy Father, you have given me your name; now protect them by the power of your name so that they will be united just as we are." John 17:11 (NLT)*

God's name kept holy in us through Christ: At Jesus' death and resurrection where He would "depart from this world," we were united with Jesus, just as He and His Father are united as One. Only while on the cross was Jesus ever separated from His Father, fulfilling the rescue mission, so we could be united as one with Him. Jesus became sin for us as if He were the one unholy, but the unholy ones were clothed in His holiness through the sacrifice of the Son of God. "For God's will was for us to be made holy by the sacrifice of the body of Jesus Christ, once for all time" (Hebrews 10:10).

> *"When he appeared in human form, he humbled himself in obedience to God and died a criminal's death on a cross. ⁹ Therefore, God elevated him to the place of highest honor and gave*

him the name above all other names." Philippians 2:8-9 (NLT)

"May your Kingdom come soon. May your will be done on earth, as it is in heaven." Matthew 6:10 (NLT)

Question 2: Please fill in the blanks. "May _____ _____ come soon. May _____ _____ be done on earth, as it is in heaven." (Matthew 6:10 NLT).

God's will is done perfectly in heaven and Jesus calls us to pray that God's will be done "on earth" as it is "in heaven." That His kingdom would reign, bringing healing and hope just as it does in heaven.

How would God bring His Kingdom to earth so His will could be done on it? God brought His kingdom to earth through Jesus' sinless sacrifice on the cross. It was the only possible way for God's will to be done on earth as it is in heaven. Jesus' miracles were the sign pointing to the work He would accomplish on the cross and proof that the "Kingdom of God has arrived among you." *"But if I am casting out demons by the power of God, then the Kingdom of God has arrived among you" (Luke 11:20 NLT).*

"Give us today the food we need," Matthew 6:11 (NLT)

Next, we see our complete dependence upon God to supply or give us the "food we need." This food is found at the cross where we see Jesus, the bread that came down from heaven, *"I am the living bread that came down from heaven. Anyone who eats this bread will live forever; and this bread, which I will offer so the world may live, is my flesh" (John 6:51).*

And this food we need is daily; Just as we need to eat daily for our physical bodies, God supplies the daily food for us spiritually. This is not food that we work for, receive from a neighbor, family member or friend, but like children who are dependent on their mother and father to care and supply for their needs, only God is able to supply the daily food we need through the Son He gave.

Question 3: While Jesus was teaching us how to pray, what is the daily food we need and how would God offer it so the world may live?

- ☐ Jesus offering His flesh on the cross, the bread from heaven, is the food we need to live.
- ☐ Jesus feeding the five thousand is the same food we need.
- ☐ Jesus would supply manna just like God did for the Israelites.

Daily we come to the cross for the spiritual food we need. Daily we come to the cross and remember our sins have been removed. Daily we see the glory of God in the face of Jesus Christ that feeds and nourishes us just as it saves and sanctifies us. *"Your ancestors ate manna in the wilderness, but they all died.* [50] *Anyone who eats the bread from heaven, however, will never die" (John 6:49-50).*

> *"...and forgive us our sins, as we have forgiven those who sin against us." Matthew 6:12 (NLT)*

Question 4: According to Matthew 6:12 what has already been done when anyone sins against us? As we have…

- ☐ Forgotten those who sin against us.
- ☐ Forsaken those who sin against us.
- ☐ Forgiven those who sin against us.

What a strange way to teach believers how to pray. We are to seek God's forgiveness as we "have forgiven" those who have sinned against us. What? How can we forgive those who sin against us before we've been forgiven? Well, we can't, only in hearing, seeing and believing by faith the message of the cross—Jesus' death and resurrection for the forgiveness of sins are we able to forgive others. We extend this forgiveness to others who have sinned against us because God has forgiven our debts, took our sins away and judged them in the Son He loves who died in our place. Jesus was treated as if He were not the Son of God on the cross filled with our sin so He could adopt us as his very own children.

"But when the right time came, God sent his Son, born of a woman, subject to the law. ⁵God sent him to buy freedom for us who were slaves to the law, so that he could adopt us as his very own children." Galatians 4:4-5 (NLT)

"And don't let us yield to temptation, but rescue us from the evil one." Matthew 6:13 (NLT)

Finally, we are pleading with our Father not to let our flesh yield to the temptation that may have overpowered us in the past; the temptation that has led us astray, the temptation that has kept us in slavery to sins sickness and power and the Tempter who deceives the world.

Question 5: How wonderful that the cross would remove sin's temptation "from us" and at the same time "rescue us" from the evil one. Please share your thoughts here.

_____

_____

_____

_____

Friend, the cross is where Jesus died to remove sins power and passion out of your heart. The place Jesus received His Father's name and kept it holy and where the will of God was made possible through the sacrifice of the Son. Jesus was broken like the bread that came from heaven to give us the food we need each day and where we receive the forgiveness of sins. But Jesus received all the arrows as God's penalty and wrath for our sin, tempted in every way but without sin, and defeated the evil one who has tried to lead us astray!

"You were dead because of your sins and because your sinful nature was not yet cut away. Then God made you alive with Christ, for he forgave all our sins. ¹⁴ He canceled the record of

the charges against us and took it away by nailing it to the cross.
¹⁵ In this way, he disarmed the spiritual rulers and authorities.
He shamed them publicly by his victory over them on the cross."
Colossians 2:14-15 (NLT)

The cross is so powerful that if we are praying cross-centered prayers we are praying according to the will of God on earth as it is in heaven. Jesus is teaching us how to pray the gospel in such a way that we would always remember it. Not praying to be seen. Not praying with babbling or vain repetition like the Gentiles do. But to pray with power to affect our lives, all believers, and the world in which we live.

Now notice how Jesus concludes His teaching on prayer, with the need to forgive how we've been forgiven. And in Christ, through His death and resurrection, our mountain of sin was completely wiped out and cast into the sea of forgetfulness. Friend, while Jesus was on the cross God was extending His compassion to us but His judgment and wrath on Jesus who absorbed the wave of punishment for our mountain of sin. *"You will again have compassion on us; you will tread our sins underfoot and hurl all our iniquities into the depths of the sea." Micah 7:19*

> *"If you forgive those who sin against you, your heavenly Father*
> *will forgive you. ¹⁵ But if you refuse to forgive others, your Father*
> *will not forgive your sins." Matthew 6:14-15*

Look at Calvary's hill where Jesus was crushed underfoot and hurled into the darkness, and where our sins were pardoned in God's compassion. Oh see the forgiveness and grace given to you but withheld from God's only Son! Oh, friend, doesn't this give you a new desire to pray for others and forgive as God has forgiven you?

Question 6: Jesus taught us how to have our prayers filled with power while being focused on the cross so that the church grows and matures in faith and forgiveness. Please share your final thoughts on this lesson.

The Gospel foretold by Moses and the Prophets

reetings, friend! Welcome back.

Today, we'll see how the Old Testament Scriptures proclaim Jesus Christ and Him crucified. It is essential to understand that when we preach and teach the message of the cross, Jesus' death and resurrection, we are "*saying nothing beyond what the prophets and Moses said would come to pass*" (Acts 26:22).

In the book of Acts the Apostle Paul was brought before the governing authorities, King Agrippa and Porcius Festus. You may remember how Paul was proclaiming how the Lord Jesus met him on the road to Damascus, where he was rescued from a "religion of works," to being "crucified with Christ." This revelation completely transformed his life from "working for salvation" into a life of resting in the finished work of Jesus crucified and His victorious resurrection. And now on trial, based on some false accusations brought against him by the Jews. Paul recounts his conversion before the Roman leader, Festus, and King Agrippa.

Let's see how the gospel is our offense/defense and the only message we have to proclaim to the church and to the world for the forgiveness of sins. Let's listen and learn from the prophets of old, how believing the good news of Christ's death and resurrection is the only hope we have to see captives set free to live in the power of God.

> "*Then I asked, 'Who are you, Lord?'* " " *I am Jesus, whom you are persecuting,' the Lord replied. 'Now get up and stand on your feet. I have appeared to you to appoint you as a servant and as a witness of what you have seen and will see of me. I will rescue you*

from your own people and from the Gentiles. I am sending you to them to open their eyes and turn them from darkness to light, and from the power of Satan to God, so that they may receive forgiveness of sins and a place among those who are sanctified by faith in me.' Acts 26:15-18 (NIV)

Question 1: According to Acts 26:16 NIV, what events happened during this encounter with the resurrected Jesus?

_____

_____

_____

_____

The Gospel Reveals: Jesus appeared and revealed Himself to Paul, even as the gospel of Jesus Christ reveals Jesus to us. *"But when God, who set me apart from my mother's womb and called me by his grace, was pleased to reveal his Son to me so that I might preach him among the Gentiles, my immediate response was not to consult any human being"* (Galatians 1:15-16).

The Gospel Appoints: Jesus appointed Paul as a servant and a witness, even as Jesus, through the amazingly good news of His death and resurrection, appoints us to proclaim the message and bear fruit. *"You did not choose me, but I chose you and appointed you so that you might go and bear fruit—fruit that will last—and so that whatever you ask in my name the Father will give you"* (John 15:16).

The Gospel Creates Entrusted Servants: *"This, then, is how you ought to regard us: as servants of Christ and as those entrusted with the mysteries God has revealed"* (1 Corinthians 4:1).

The Gospel Sends Witnesses: *"But you will receive power when the Holy Spirit comes on you, and you will be my witnesses in Jerusalem, and in all Judea and Samaria, and to the ends of the earth"* (Acts 1:8). *"He said to them, "Go into all the world and preach the gospel to all creation"* (Mark 16:15).

"...to open their eyes and turn them from darkness to light, and from the power of Satan to God, so that they may receive forgiveness of sins and a place among those who are sanctified by faith in me." Acts 26:18 (NIV)

Question 2: According to Acts 26:18 NIV, what was the purpose that Jesus revealed Himself to us and appointed us as servants and witnesses of His gospel?

Friend, the cross is where Jesus reveals Himself to us by "*opening our eyes*", turning all who believe "*from darkness to light*", and from "*the power of Satan to God*". The cross is where we find forgiveness of sins and a place among other believers who are being sanctified in Christ. The cross is the place we have "seen" and will "see" more of Jesus as He reveals more of Himself to us who are being sanctified by faith in Christ. "I have appeared to you to appoint you as a servant and as a witness of what you have seen and will see of me" (Acts 26:16). Preaching and teaching the gospel in the church is the most important thing we can do, as it is the most powerful message in the world. We want to proclaim the gospel message clearly so that eyes are opened wide to the glories of Calvary. We want to see more and more of the light of Jesus so that our hearts are continually turning from darkness to Christ, the Light of the world (John 8:12).

Notice how Paul completes his testimony:

"That is why some Jews seized me in the temple courts and tried to kill me. But God has helped me to this very day; so I stand here and testify to small and great alike. I am saying nothing beyond what the prophets and Moses said would happen— that the Messiah would suffer and, as the first to rise from the dead,

would bring the message of light to his own people and to the Gentiles." Acts 26:21-23 (NIV)

Question 3: Please fill in the blanks: "so I stand here and _____ to small and great alike. I am saying _____ beyond what the _____ and _____ _____ would happen" (Acts 26:22 NIV).

Question 4: According to Acts 26:23, what did Moses and the prophets say would happen?
- ☐ That Jesus would liberate the Jews from Roman oppression by leading a military conquest.
- ☐ That Jesus would show the Jews how to keep God's Laws correctly.
- ☐ That Jesus would suffer, die and be the first to rise from the dead.

The only message we proclaim to both small and great is, *"saying nothing beyond what the prophets and Moses said would happen."* The message they proclaimed was clear: that Jesus would suffer and die for the forgiveness of sins and be the first to rise from the dead on the third day. This message is rooted in the Old Testament Scriptures: *"For what I received I passed on to you as of first importance: that Christ died for our sins according to the Scriptures, that he was buried, that he was raised on the third day according to the Scriptures." 1 Corinthians 15:3-4 (NIV)* This is the good news we now proclaim to all. Some will believe, have their sins forgiven, be raised to live new lives. They will begin to walk in the light that has shone into their darkened hearts, will walk in the power of the Spirit they received by believing the message of the cross. Still, others may think we are out of our minds as the cross is foolishness to them (1 Corinthians 1:18).

Notice Festus' response to Paul: *"At this point, Festus interrupted Paul's defense. "You are out of your mind, Paul!" he shouted. "Your great learning is driving you insane." "I am not insane, most excellent Festus," Paul replied. "What I am saying is true and reasonable. The king is familiar with these things, and I can speak freely to him. I am convinced that none of this has escaped his notice, because it was not done in a corner." Acts 26:24-26 (NIV)*

> **Question 5:** While he proclaimed that Christ had to suffer for our sins and be the first to rise from the dead for our justification, what accusation was made against Paul?
> ☐ He was a loose cannon and in need of help.
> ☐ He was very wise and speaking a powerful message.
> ☐ He was out of his mind and insane.

Paul now brings the conclusion of the matter before these two governing authorities, asking them to consider the gospel and respond appropriately by believing the message:

> *"King Agrippa, do you believe the prophets? I know you do." Then Agrippa said to Paul, "Do you think that in such a short time you can persuade me to be a Christian?" Paul replied, "Short time or long—I pray to God that not only you but all who are listening to me today may become what I am, except for these chains." Acts 26:27-29 (NIV)*

By proclaiming the gospel message to both small and great, we are proclaiming *"nothing beyond what the prophets and Moses said would happen"* (v22), sharing both the Scriptures and our transformation stories about the power of the cross.

By proclaiming the gospel message we are speaking "true and reasonable" words (v25)

By proclaiming the gospel message we are asking our hearers to believe the message, turn from Satan to God, from darkness to light, receive forgiveness of their sins and embrace the amazing transformation that looking to the cross always brings: *"Short time or long—I pray to God that not only you but all who are listening to me today may become what I am"* (v29)

Question 6: What are your thoughts on proclaiming the gospel? Do you have any struggles or questions about proclaiming the gospel as described in this lesson? Please share.

_____

_____

_____

_____

Friend, let us continue to proclaim the message of the cross within the church to both small and great, saying nothing but what the prophets and Moses said would happen. And praying for all, whether it takes a short or a long time, that those who hear the gospel message might meet their own death and resurrection and experience the power of the gospel, have their eyes opened, their sins forgiven. This means they will be removed out of the darkness and the "power of Satan to God" and find true and lasting freedom, healing in Jesus' wounds, and lifelong joy of walking in the Spirit!

As we bring this lesson to a close let's do so by looking at what the prophets and Moses said would come to pass and see how all Scripture points to the coming Messiah's suffering; "*that the Messiah would suffer and, as the first to rise from the dead, would bring the message of light to his own people and to the Gentiles*" (Acts 26:23 NIV). Notice the following passages of Scripture and see the powerful message of the cross/resurrection of Jesus:

> "*For Moses said, 'The Lord your God will raise up for you a prophet like me from among your own people; you must listen to everything he tells you*" (Deuteronomy 18:15 NIV).

> "*Then God said, "Take your son, your only son, whom you love—Isaac—and go to the region of Moriah. Sacrifice him there as a burnt offering on a mountain I will show you*" (Genesis 22:2 NIV).

Because of His great love for us, God's only Son came to this dark world and lived a perfect and sinless life before God the Father. He then went to the cross and offered His back to those who beat Him, His cheeks to those who pulled out His beard; He did not hide His face from mocking and spitting (Isaiah 50:6 NIV). He came as "the True Light" for those walking in darkness (bondage to sin and unbelief), and through His substitutionary death, He forgave our sin and nailed it to the cross, shining the light of God's favor on all who believe this message (Isaiah 9:2).

> "They will look on me, the one they have pierced, and they will mourn for him as one mourns for an only child, and grieve bitterly for him as one grieves for a firstborn son" (Zechariah 12:10 NIV).

> "In that day," declares the Sovereign Lord, "I will make the sun go down at noon and darken the earth in broad daylight. I will turn your religious festivals into mourning and all your singing into weeping. I will make all of you wear sackcloth and shave your heads. I will make that time like mourning for an only son and the end of it like a bitter day" (Amos 8:9-10 NIV).

> "I am poured out like water, and all my bones are out of joint. My heart has turned to wax; it has melted within me. My mouth is dried up like a potsherd, and my tongue sticks to the roof of my mouth; you lay me in the dust of death. Dogs surround me, a pack of villains encircles me; they pierce my hands and my feet" (Psalm 22:14-16 NIV).

> "Just as there were many who were appalled at him— his appearance was so disfigured beyond that of any human being and his form marred beyond human likeness" (Isaiah 52:14 NIV).

> "he was pierced for our transgressions, he was crushed for our iniquities; the punishment that brought us peace was on him, and by his wounds we are healed" (Isaiah 53:5); He was pierced and suffered but will bind up our wounds with His nail-pierced hands and "After two days he will revive us; on the third day he will restore us, that we may live in his presence" (Hosea 6:1-3 NIV).

Dear friend, this is the love of God stretched out and held on the cross for you! This is the love of God pierced and stricken for you! Sin is so ugly that God poured out His entire wrath on His own beloved Son so we could live in His presence forgiven and free from sin's power!

This is the message we proclaim in our churches that many more may die with Christ and be raised to live new lives free from sins slavery and Satan's power, having turned from the power of Satan to God Acts 26:18 (NIV).

> *"So a time was set, and on that day a large number of people came to Paul's lodging. He explained and testified about the Kingdom of God and tried to persuade them about Jesus from the Scriptures. Using the law of Moses and the books of the prophets, he spoke to them from morning until evening." Acts 28:23 (NLT)*

> *"...that the Messiah would suffer and, as the first to rise from the dead, would bring the message of light to his own people and to the Gentiles" (Acts 26:23).*

Question 7: When we are preaching, teaching a bible study or Sunday school class we are "saying nothing beyond what the prophets and Moses said would come to pass." How might this lesson help the church to focus on the message of power to crucify and raise to life? Please share your thoughts.

The Cross is Our Red Sea

*T*oday we want to see an amazing picture that God gave us to reveal the cross. It is the story of the Passover Lamb saving the lives of the Israelites, then setting them free from slavery, and what happened shortly after that event. This story is given to us specifically that we might "see" the salvation of the Lord.

As you know the Israelites were freed from their miserable life of slavery by slaughtering a lamb and applying the blood to the doorposts (Exodus 12:7). Now escaping with all the treasure gathered from the Egyptians and free from their 430 years of slavery they come up to the Red Sea.

The Red Sea was ahead of them and Pharoah and his army came after them. You can hear the Egyptian chariots thundering, the horses galloping and the earth rumbling under their feet as the army was closing in on God's people.

> *"When Pharaoh drew near, the people of Israel lifted up their eyes, and behold, the Egyptians were marching after them, and they feared greatly. And the people of Israel cried out to the Lord. 11 They said to Moses, "Is it because there are no graves in Egypt that you have taken us away to die in the wilderness? What have you done to us in bringing us out of Egypt? 12 Is not this what we said to you in Egypt: 'Leave us alone that we may serve the Egyptians'? For it would have been better for us to serve the Egyptians than to die in the wilderness." Exodus 14:10-12*

Question 1: According to Exodus 14:10-12, why were the Israelites afraid of the Egyptian army after being freed from their miserable years of slavery?

☐ They lifted up their thoughts and prayed.

☐ They lifted up their eyes and saw the army marching after them.

☐ They lifted up their hearts before the Lord and did not worry about the army.

Question 2: According to Exodus 14:12, what did the Israelites think would be better than their freedom?

☐ Returning to their homeland rather than living in the wilderness.

☐ Returning to the land of plenty rather than living with nothing.

☐ Returning to the bitter land of slavery rather than dying in the wilderness.

This is what the enemy tries to do to the church, also; he attempts to drive us back into the land of slavery rather than us taking the escape route the Lord has already laid out. We lift up our eyes and see the enemy and become filled with fear, and we despair of ever finding true freedom. The Israelites had the enemy on one side and the Red Sea on the other, and they could see no possible escape route.

Is it because there are no graves in Egypt that you have taken us away to die in the wilderness? They knew it was over! What have you done to us in bringing us out of Egypt? They would rather go back to the land of slavery than to die in the wilderness. Is not this what we said to you in Egypt: "Leave us alone that we may serve the Egyptians'? For it would have been better for us to serve the Egyptians than to die in the wilderness."

"And Moses said to the people, "Fear not, stand firm, and see the salvation of the Lord, which he will work for you today. For the Egyptians whom you see today, you shall never see again. ¹⁴ The Lord will fight for you, and you have only to be silent." Exodus 14:13-14

Question 3: Please list everything the Israelites were told to do or would experience from Exodus 14:13-14.

_____

_____

_____

_____

Look at the promises! Wow, what comfort and love the Lord has for His people! What a word that came from the Lord ready not only to demonstrate His great and mighty power for His people against their enemies but displaying His great love for His son Israel.

Likewise, God sent His Son, The Lamb of God who was slain to provide blood on the doorposts of our hearts, to inaugurate the Passover celebration. God's firstborn Son was "struck down" and poured out unto death on the cross to remove God's judgment, destroy all our idols, and save us from wrath. "... *take some of the blood and put it on the sides and tops of the doorframes of the houses where they eat the lambs (Exodus 12:7). "On that same night I will pass through Egypt and strike down every firstborn of both people and animals, and I will bring judgment on all the gods of Egypt. I am the LORD" (Exodus 12:12).* God took them out of Egypt with a mighty hand and outstretched arm not to let them be overtaken in the wilderness but to take them to the promised land.

> *"You brought your people Israel out of the land of Egypt with signs and wonders, with a strong hand and outstretched arm, and with great terror" Jeremiah 32:21*

The Lord said to the Israelites:
- FEAR NOT
- STAND FIRM
- SEE the SALVATION of the Lord
- He will WORK for you TODAY
- The Egyptians whom you SEE TODAY
- You shall NEVER SEE again

- The Lord will FIGHT FOR YOU
- You have only to BE SILENT

God wanted the Israelites not to fear but to stand firm and "SEE" the salvation of the Lord. Watch ME work again! Look how I'm caring for you! Don't miss what I'm about to do! I will work on your behalf! You will "NEVER SEE" these enemies again! I will fight for you while you are standing firm and silent!

> *"Then Moses stretched out his hand over the sea, and the Lord drove the sea back by a strong east wind all night and made the sea dry land, and the waters were divided. ²² And the people of Israel went into the midst of the sea on dry ground, the waters being a wall to them on their right hand and on their left ²³ The Egyptians pursued and went in after them into the midst of the sea, all Pharaoh's horses, his chariots, and his horsemen. ²⁴ And in the morning watch the Lord in the pillar of fire and of cloud looked down on the Egyptian forces and threw the Egyptian forces into a panic, ²⁵ clogging their chariot wheels so that they drove heavily. And the Egyptians said, "Let us flee from before Israel, for the Lord fights for them against the Egyptians." Exodus 14:21-25*

Question 4: Even the Egyptians saw God's power; they understood that God was fighting for the Israelites and against themselves.
  ☐ True
  ☐ False

Friend, on the cross Jesus stretched out his hands, gave up His life and poured out blood like the Red Sea, putting our enemy to death, baptizing us into His death, buying our way out of the slave market while He, Himself, was nailed like a slave to the cross. The Lord drove the Red Sea of our sin back with His hands while delivering us from our sin slavery. The cross is our dry and stable ground where we are able to "stand firm", and it keeps us from sinking back into the deep waters of sin. We've all experienced wave after wave of sins power over us, but when Jesus was on the cross the waters of our sin were divided and we walked through on dry ground, were baptized into Christ's death, buried with Him in the grave and were raised with Christ from the dead by the power of God.

> *"Do you not know that all of us who have been baptized into Christ Jesus were baptized into his death? ⁴We were buried therefore with him by baptism into death, in order that, just as Christ was raised from the dead by the glory of the Father, we too might walk in newness of life" (Romans 6:3-4.*

> *"Then the Lord said to Moses, "Stretch out your hand over the sea, that the water may come back upon the Egyptians, upon their chariots, and upon their horsemen." ²⁷ So Moses stretched out his hand over the sea, and the sea returned to its normal course when the morning appeared. And as the Egyptians fled into it, the Lord threw the Egyptians into the midst of the sea. ²⁸ The waters returned and covered the chariots and the horsemen; of all the host of Pharaoh that had followed them into the sea, not one of them remained. ²⁹ But the people of Israel walked on dry ground" Exodus 14:26-29*

> *"I called forth the mighty army of Egypt with all its chariots and horses. I drew them beneath the waves, and they drowned, their lives snuffed out like a smoldering candlewick" (Isaiah 43:17).*

The Red Sea cut off the route back to the land of Egypt where there was nothing but bitter labor, miserable living, slavery, and death. As we keep our eyes fixed on the cross we see our fear wiped out, knowing that we can stand firm and see the victory and salvation of the Lord. We do nothing but watch God work through Jesus who took the punishment for our sins and whose blood flowed like a flood to save us and set us free from our land of slavery and baptize us in the Red Sea of His love. The cross blocks our way back to slavery, showing us that we died to that life in the body of Jesus Christ, and have risen to new life, on the other shore.

"Give thanks to him who parted the Red Sea. His faithful love endures forever. ¹⁴ He led Israel safely through, His faithful love endures forever. ¹⁵ but he hurled Pharaoh and his army into the Red Sea. His faithful love endures forever. ¹⁶ Give thanks to him who led his people through the wilderness. His faithful love endures forever" (Psalm 136:13-16 NLT).

"For I do not want you to be unaware, brothers, that our fathers were all under the cloud, and all passed through the sea, ² and all were baptized into Moses in the cloud and in the sea" (1 Corinthians 10:1-2).

Question 5: Have you seen the cross and all its wondrous, marvelous, and glorious power today? Please share your thoughts.

_____

_____

_____

_____

"Thus the Lord saved Israel that day from the hand of the Egyptians, and Israel saw the Egyptians dead on the seashore. ³¹ Israel saw the great power that the Lord used against the Egyptians, so the people feared the Lord, and they believed in the Lord and in his servant Moses." Exodus 14:30-31

The Lord wanted the Israelites to SEE the salvation of the Lord. He wanted them to SEE the enemy dead on the seashore. And He wanted them to SEE the great power the Lord was "for them" but "against their enemy." Like Jesus when He lifted up His arms to save and sanctify us but "disarmed the powers and authorities, he made a public spectacle of them, triumphing over them by the cross" (Colossians 2:15).

Jesus was under the waves of the Red Sea as they came crashing down on Him, crushing Him as He was gasping for one more breath to save one more life, wave after wave of God's judgment engulfed Him. Oh, friend, when you look to the cross do you see the salvation of the Lord? Do you see the enemy defeated but the great power of the Lord working for you? Look at Jesus on that cross dying for you, healing you with His wounds and rising to life to save and sanctify the church beneath His cleansing flood.

Question 6: How will the illustration in this lesson provide hope, encouragement, and strengthen the church? Reminding all that the escape route is through the Red Sea where Jesus went up Calvary's hill, stretched out His arms and shed His blood in the Rea Sea providing God's forgiveness, love, mercy, and grace to us, and the way of escape from sins slavery and power?

Man's Steps Up Vs. Jesus' Steps Down

MAN ATTEMPTS TO STEP UP

Greetings, friend, and welcome! Today, we will be contrasting man's religious efforts through the steps he takes to Jesus' stepping down into death for us.

By default, humans try to establish a righteousness of their own. It is what all people apart from Christ do. They make their programs for self-improvement with various steps, rules, and laws. Their thinking is that if they keep taking the next step that they will better themselves, make themselves right, even be right with God; that is, they will reach heaven! But the Bible tells us that there is only one way to God.

Today, we will consider two passages of Scripture, which will illuminate this issue for us. At the end of the lesson, there will be only one question to allow you the opportunity to summarize the teaching and share your thoughts:

The first Scripture passage is Genesis 11:1-4, and it says:

> *"Now the whole world had one language and a common speech. 2 As people moved eastward, they found a plain in Shinar and settled there. 3 They said to each other, (by the way they didn't ask God) "Come, let's make bricks and bake them thoroughly." They used brick instead of stone, and tar for mortar. 4 Then they said, "Come, let us build ourselves a city, with a tower that reaches to the heavens so that we may make a name for ourselves; otherwise we will be scattered over the face of the whole earth."*
> *Genesis 11:1-4 (NIV)*

Here we read that God told the people to scatter over the face of the whole earth, but the people had other plans. In building their tower, they were rebelling against God. They were literally trying to build their way up to God in heaven. They were trying to put step upon step, brick upon brick until their tower reached heaven.

And this is always man's way; this is the world's way; this is how Satan wants to blind us to the message of the cross. Satan wants to get us to think about working our way 'up.' This is why every religion in the world focuses on the individual working their way 'up' to God.

So, in Genesis 11, we find a group of proud, industrious people who want to make a name for themselves by reaching God in heaven through their own efforts.

JESUS STEPS DOWN

Now let's consider Philippians 2:6-8:

> [Jesus] "Who, being in very nature God, did not consider equality with God something to be used to his own advantage; rather, he made himself nothing by taking the very nature of a servant, being made in human likeness. And being found in appearance as a man, he humbled himself by becoming obedient to death—even death on a cross!" Philippians 2:6-8 (NIV)

Here we see Jesus, the Lord of Glory, and His way of making us right with God. Look how far down Jesus kept going, look how low He continued to go, step after step after step, downward he went. The almighty God became a man; the perfect man became a servant, the servant humbled Himself to die as a criminal on a cross. Why? He died to raise you to a new life in Him. He came to earth to bring you to heaven; He died on a cross to make you righteous before God. He came down to lift you up.

It's interesting in Genesis 11, the people wanted to make a name for themselves, by going higher and higher. But Jesus, by going lower and lower, was given *"the name that is above every name, that at the name of Jesus every knee should bow, in heaven and on earth and under the earth, and every tongue acknowledge that Jesus Christ is Lord, to the glory of God the Father." Philippians 2:9-11 (NIV)*

So, what can we learn from this contrast? First of all, we see the amazing length to which Jesus went. He just couldn't seem to go low enough for us: from heaven to earth, from God to man, from man to a servant, from a servant to being treated as a criminal. Jesus went from heaven to hell. He kept going lower for us. He couldn't go any lower than He went taking your sin upon Himself, wrapping it around himself like a garment.

He went to the cross, was stripped naked except for the garment of our sins, nails were pounded into His hands and feet, a crown of thorns was placed upon His head, and a soldier stabbed his heart and out came blood and water, and there He hung His head and died.

Jesus went to the lowest depths to raise you and me up to the highest heights of heaven, to save us from sin's penalty, to rescue us from sin's power, to redeem us from the curse of the law, and to make us righteous.

We could not do it; therefore, God did it for us. He made us righteous; He made it so that we who live by the Spirit are considered as if we have kept the full law (Romans 8:3). Why? Because Jesus was treated as a lawbreaker. Jesus was treated like a criminal that we might be counted righteous. What a Savior!

When we contrast the people in Genesis 11 with Jesus in Philippians 2, we can see the tremendous difference between man's ways and God's. Man focuses on working the steps, trying to climb higher, and God's way was to send His Son ever lower to the point of going to Sheol for you and me, to raise us up, to take us out of the pit, to release us from the chains, to break our iron chains, to open our prison doors, and to set us free.

I encourage you today (if you haven't already) to turn away from all of man's methods, from working your way anywhere, from working programs, and instead receive the glorious gifts of God through Christ. Receive the grace of the cross and the power of the Spirit that raises us and takes us out of sin and brings us to heaven where we worship the name that is above every name, the name of Jesus.

Thank you so much, Jesus, for how You lowered Yourself, for how far down You went to rescue us, for the lengths that You went like a waterfall going lower and lower. And now, Lord, help us to have Your mind, going lower and lower, seeking to humble ourselves into servanthood. Make us to give of ourselves, to give our lives away even as You did. Thank You, Jesus, Amen.

Question 1: Please contrast man's way vs. God's way, using Genesis 11:1-4 and Philippians 2:6-11 as reference points and share any thoughts you have about this contrast.

Confidence in The Cross removes Confidence in The Flesh

Welcome back, friend. Today we're going to compare human achievements and confidence in the flesh, to the finished work of Christ.

The Apostle Paul had many "human achievements" he could have trusted in, but instead, he was laser-focused on Jesus' death and resurrection. In his introduction and opening statement in Galatians 1, he immediately wanted his readers to understand one thing, that his new life in Christ did not come from men or his own efforts, but his heart change came through Jesus' death and resurrection power. *"Paul, an apostle—not from men nor through man, but through Jesus Christ and God the Father, who raised him from the dead-" (Galatians 1:1).*

> *"For it is we who are the circumcision, we who serve God by his Spirit, who boast in Christ Jesus, and who put no confidence in the flesh" (Philippians 3:3 NIV).*

Did you notice the connection? Being circumcised in our hearts is also how we serve God through His Spirit, how we walk by the Spirit. Paul, did, however, go on to say that if anyone could boast in the flesh it would be him:

> *"though I myself have reasons for such confidence. If someone else thinks they have reasons to put confidence in the flesh, I have more: circumcised on the eighth day, of the people of Israel, of the tribe of Benjamin, a Hebrew of Hebrews; in regard to the law, a Pharisee; as for zeal, persecuting the church; as for righteousness based on the law, faultless" (Philippians 3:4-6 NIV).*

Question 1: Please fill in the blanks: "For it is ____ who are the _____, we who _____ _____ by his Spirit, who _____ in Christ _____, and who put _____ _____ in the _____" (Philippians 3:3).

Confidence in the cross removes confidence in the flesh! In other words, Paul at one time boasted about his knowledge, accomplishments, and how he was advancing far beyond those of his own age (Galatians 1:14). In Paul's former life and religion, he was zealous and faultless, but it was based upon "confidence in the flesh" and that is what he could boast about. But now he boasts in his new life in Christ where his heart was circumcised by the Spirit of God which transformed him from one who "boasts in the flesh" to "boasting in the cross."

> *"May I never boast except in the cross of our Lord Jesus Christ, through which the world has been crucified to me, and I to the world." (Galatians 6:14 NIV)*

Prior to Paul's conversation he had zeal and passion, he was faultless through the law and he eagerly desired to be right with God. But look at what his "religious zeal" and "faultless" living produced.

> *"as for zeal, persecuting the church; as for righteousness based on the law, faultless" (Philippians 3:6 NIV).*

Question 2: What did Paul's religion and righteousness drive him to do to the church? And what was his primary focus in his thinking (v6)?
- ☐ He encouraged the church, even though he thought himself to be a sinner.
- ☐ He persecuted the church and thought he was faultless according to the law.
- ☐ He loved the church and never thought about persecuting it at all.

Friend, we want to see Jesus lifted up on the cross pierced in His heart to transform ours, and we want to be putting "faith" in the message of the cross and "confidence" in Jesus Christ crucified rather than confidence in the flesh. We are not those who want to put confidence in the flesh listing out what WE have done or what WE do, but rather we put confidence in Jesus' flesh that was crucified for us, boasting in the list of what Christ HAS already done for us when He was crucified.

Faith comes through "hearing" the message of the cross: *"So faith comes from hearing, and hearing through the word of Christ"* (Romans 10:17).

"Hearing" with faith the message of the cross is how we receive the Spirit: *"Let me ask you only this: Did you receive the Spirit by works of the law or by hearing with faith?" (Galatians 3:2)*

Faith in the death and resurrection of Christ brings a washing, rebirth, and renewal by the Holy Spirit: *"he saved us, not because of righteous things we had done, but because of his mercy. He saved us through the washing of rebirth and renewal by the Holy Spirit," (Titus 3:5)*

What man, or group of men, could we hear from that would change our lives? What other messages could we hear by which we would receive God's Spirit? From who or where could we go to receive mercy, salvation, washing, rebirth, and renewal by the Holy Spirit?

Our lives are no longer under the written code instituted by the finger of God and written on tablets of stone, but rather we are under a New Covenant given by "nail-pierced hands" written with the blood of Jesus on tablets of human hearts.

> *"You show that you are a letter from Christ, the result of our ministry, written not with ink but with the Spirit of the living God, not on tablets of stone but on tablets of human hearts"* (2 Corinthians 3:3 NIV).

No group of men or any man could ever offer this gift to you and me.

Please look to the cross now: can you hear the nails being driven into your sin through Jesus' flesh? Can you see the blood of Jesus staining the wooden post with every strike of the nail? Can you see every strike to His face by the fists of evil men? Can you see Jesus pouring out His life like a fountain? Can

SETTING CAPTIVES FREE

you see Jesus being put to death on the cross for you as the crowd gathered around not to weep for their sins nor the death of their Savior, but to cheer His death yelling "Crucify Him!?" "Crucify Him!?"

> **Question 3:** Can you hear the sound of the nails being driven into Jesus' hands and feet, blows to His face, the striking of Jesus' head over and over as He went to the cross to pardon your sin and pay your debt? Please share your thoughts.

Paul continued to show the transformation that took place in his life as the reason he considered his gain as loss and the reason for his ongoing pursuit of Christ. He described how he was transferred from the kingdom of darkness to the Kingdom of light, from a "persecutor of the church" to "pursuer of Christ." At the cross, Paul was transformed into a preacher of the gospel. He now saw his mission was to love the church as Christ Jesus loved him and gave Himself up for him.

> *"But whatever were gains to me I now consider loss for the sake of Christ" (Philippians 3:7 NIV).*

What gains did Paul now consider to be a loss for the sake of Christ? All the knowledge Paul gained through his religious efforts, all his religious zeal, all his human achievements now considered to be a loss. Wasn't there something he could have held on to from his former religion to harmonize with Christ? All of it couldn't be thrown in the garbage, could it?

> *"What is more, I consider everything a loss because of the surpassing worth of knowing Christ Jesus my Lord, for whose*

sake I have lost all things. I consider them garbage, that I may gain Christ" (Philippians 3:8 NIV).

Question 4: According to Philippians 3:8, compared with the surpassing worth of Christ, what did Paul consider everything else?

_____

_____

_____

_____

Friend, this is the laser focus we talked about at the beginning of today's study. "Paul, an apostle—not from men nor through man, but through Jesus Christ and God the Father, who raised him from the dead-" (Galatians 1:1). Not from men nor through man, meaning there was nothing that could be carried over from his former religion. It was all a loss to him for the surpassing worth of knowing Christ.

Everything he previously thought and was taught as useful from man's point of view had now become garbage. The message of Jesus Christ and Him crucified, the power of God, is completely opposed to man's religion, human traditions, human wisdom, and human reasoning. This heart and life-transforming power at the cross is the reason we call everyone to look to the cross by faith and believe the message, for this cross alone frees captives, releases sin-prisoners, heals broken hearts, and brings true worship to all.

"See to it that no one takes you captive through hollow and deceptive philosophy, which depends on human tradition and the elemental spiritual forces of this world rather than on Christ" (Colossians 2:8 NIV).

"This is what we speak, not in words taught us by human wisdom but in words taught by the Spirit, explaining spiritual realities with Spirit-taught words" (1 Corinthians 2:13 NIV).

It's not about human tradition or wisdom, but words "taught by the Spirit." Human tradition and wisdom keeps us captive, trapped in a righteousness of our own. Freedom from sin's power comes through the Spirit of God who flowed from the powerful cross where Jesus was crucified. "Now the Lord is the Spirit, and where the Spirit of the Lord is, there is freedom" (2 Corinthians 3:17 NIV).

"and be found in him, not having a righteousness of my own that comes from the law, but that which is through faith in Christ— the righteousness that comes from God on the basis of faith" (Philippians 3:9 NIV).

Question 5: What are the two types of righteousness listed in Philippians 3:9?
- ☐ A righteousness of my own/a righteousness that comes from faith in right living.
- ☐ A righteousness of my own/a righteousness that comes through working hard.
- ☐ A righteousness of my own/a righteousness that comes through faith in Christ.

"For I can testify about them that they are zealous for God, but their zeal is not based on knowledge. ³Since they did not know the righteousness of God and sought to establish their own, they did not submit to God's righteousness" Romans 10:2-3 NIV.

"I want to know Christ—yes, to know the power of his resurrection and participation in his sufferings, becoming like him in his death, and so, somehow, attaining to the resurrection from the dead." Philippians 3:10-11 NIV.

Can you see the connection between the two statements "to know Christ" and "to know the power" of His resurrection? Paul here wants to participate in the sufferings of Christ, the death of Christ and thereby joining Christ in the resurrection from the dead. What a contrast from a "righteousness of my own", to the righteousness found only in Christ. To know the power of Jesus' resurrection is to know Christ in a personal way through our new life experience. At the cross, our hearts are pierced, as Jesus' heart was, and we experience amazing burning in our pierced hearts to know Him more. Paul said, "I want to know Christ!"

Question 6: What about you, friend, do you have a law-based righteousness of your own, or righteousness that comes from God on the basis of faith in Christ?
- ☐ I have been living as though I can obtain righteousness through the law.
- ☐ I have the righteousness of Christ through faith in His death and resurrection through the power of God.

"All of us, then, who are mature should take such a view of things. And if on some point you think differently, that too God will make clear to you" Philippians 3:15 NIV

"For, as I have often told you before and now tell you again even with tears, many live as enemies of the cross of Christ. Their destiny is destruction, their god is their stomach, and their glory is in their shame. Their mind is set on earthly things" Philippians 3:18-19 NIV.

Question 7: What is the basis for Paul's tears and the reason many live as "enemies of the cross"?
- ☐ Their mind is set on earthly things.
- ☐ Their mind is set of heavenly things.
- ☐ Their mind is set on eternal things.

Friend, may we plead with the gospel message in our churches; preaching and teaching the need to abandon all hope and confidence in the flesh, all human achievements and wisdom so that our minds will not be set on earthly things. But let us invite all to come to the cross and see Jesus removing their "confidence in the flesh" as He was pierced and cut off in His. Come and die with Jesus, and find real life!

God's Grace Abounds at The Cross

"For sin shall no longer be your master, because you are not under the law, but under grace." Romans 6:14 NIV

reetings, friend, and welcome back to the course. Today we want to see that all of humanity is under something. We are either under the law and its power, or the grace of God and the power of the cross of Christ.

And isn't it wonderful that through Jesus' sacrifice on the cross, sin shall no longer be "your master" (Romans 6:14)? Because of the cross, we are not under the weight of the law any longer! This is such good news because the law exerted power over us, pushing us under the waters of sin, down into the deepest darkness of condemnation, with all its guilt and shame.

All people are either under God's law where sins' mastery reigns or we are under God's grace, where SIN shall no longer be YOUR MASTER. Sin was "over" us pushing us "under" where we couldn't breathe, couldn't see, and couldn't find our own way out because it's weight was too heavy for us—too powerful for us.

Here's the "good news" though friend, as we look up to the cross, we see that Jesus carried the "weight" and suffered "under" the curse for us; we see that He was under the law and under the resulting judgment against us that it brought to Him. And being under the law in this way He took that which was over us and put it to death, so we could be under His blood as a protective covering. Under the grace of God. Under the One who shed His blood, gave up His robe of righteousness to us, gave up His back to be ripped apart for us, and lifted His face to be struck for us!

Jesus went "under" sins' judgment like a criminal so we could be "under" His grace like a son or daughter. Under His care! Under His healing wounds!

Under His forgiveness! Under His love! Everyone is either "under the law" or "under the grace" of God, where Jesus' blood ran red and our sins were washed white!

> *"The law was brought in so that the trespass might increase. But where sin increased, grace increased all the more, [21] so that, just as sin reigned in death, so also grace might reign through righteousness to bring eternal life through Jesus Christ our Lord." Romans 5:20-21 NIV*

When the law was "brought in" the trespass "increased." This was the very purpose of the law that the glory and grace of God might be displayed in brighter brilliance through the sacrifice of Jesus Christ, so that "grace might reign through righteousness." The grace of God, the righteousness which brings eternal life and washes us clean is found in the blood of Jesus. We were bought when blood was slain. And where this grace of God reigns, the law no longer has power over you. Isn't this good news to you? Aren't you relieved that you are no longer under the law with its power over you but under the blood of Christ?

> *"The law was brought in so that the trespass might increase. But where sin increased, grace increased all the more" Romans 5:20*

Question 1: According to Romans 5:20, where sin increased, what did God's grace do at the cross?

_____

_____

_____

_____

> *"What shall we say, then? Shall we go on sinning so that grace may increase? [2] By no means! We are those who have died to sin; how can we live in it any longer?" Romans 6:1-2 NIV*

Question 2: What is the reason believers cannot say that "God's grace" is a "license" to go on sinning?
- ☐ Believers try hard by works to die to sin.
- ☐ Believers have died to sin and no longer live in it.
- ☐ Believers are still alive to sin because we can't help it.

"For sin shall no longer be your master, because you are not under the law, but under grace. ¹⁵ What then? Shall we sin because we are not under the law but under grace? By no means!" Romans 6:14-15 NIV

Ungodly people (those who have not died and been raised with Christ) pervert the grace of God and turn it into a license to sin, and therefore, *"they have denied our only Master and Lord, Jesus Christ, who bought them" (Jude 1:4).* The message of the cross was foolish to them, reducing the grace of God to a license for further immoral living, *"having the appearance of godliness, but denying its power." 2 Timothy 3:5*

"Dear friends, I had been eagerly planning to write to you about the salvation we all share. But now I find that I must write about something else, urging you to defend the faith that God has entrusted once for all time to his holy people. ⁴ I say this because some ungodly people have wormed their way into your churches, saying that God's marvelous grace allows us to live immoral lives. The condemnation of such people was recorded long ago, for they have denied our only Master and Lord, Jesus Christ" (Jude 1:3-4 NLT).

Question 3: What message was Jude intending to deliver, but led to write and urge believers to instead defend the faith that God has entrusted to His holy people?
- ☐ About the salvation we all share and the law we must keep.
- ☐ About the salvation we all share and the freedom we have in Christ.
- ☐ About the salvation we all share and the works we must do.

Question 4: Who is it that has "wormed their way" into our churches to pervert the grace of God?

☐ The ungodly desire to live holy lives.

☐ The godly are leaving the church.

☐ The ungodly who say that the grace of God allows us to live immoral lives.

"This matter arose because some false believers had infiltrated our ranks to spy on the freedom we have in Christ Jesus and to make us slaves. ⁵ We did not give in to them for a moment, so that the truth of the gospel might be preserved for you." Galatians 2:4-5 NIV

Dear friend, we cannot give in to those who want to pervert the grace of God, whether it's turning it into a license to sin or trying to bring us back under the law and its slavery. We must "preserve the gospel" not only for future generations but also because it is the message given to the church to take into all the world. The truth of the gospel must never be perverted! And never be used as "freedom" to live in sin, because believers *"...are those who have died to sin; how can we live in it any longer?" Romans 6:2 NIV*

Jesus went under the curse, *"For all who rely on the works of the law are under a curse"* (Galatians 3:10) for us while He hung on the tree (Galatians 3:13) even though He continued to do *"everything written in the Book of the Law"* (Galatians 3:10). He is the end and fulfillment of the law (Romans 10:4). Out of love for you and me, He went to the cross where He was lifted up as a "law breaker" and "Passover Lamb" who loved us to the end of His life by hanging in our place. He was under the judgment of sin for us and received our death sentence on the cross. We were "passed over," and God's firstborn was put to death, and the first fruits rose from the dead (1 Corinthians 15:20).

If you ever wonder if God loves you, all you have to do is look to the cross of Christ and see the grace of God and the love of Jesus vividly displayed. Look at Him going to the cross and loving us to the end of His life (John 13:1). With each blow of the hammer that pounded the nails deeper into His hands and feet, He loved you. He loved you while under the agony of death where His heart was pierced, His love poured out, and with those wounds He bandaged and healed you. Jesus loved us to the end with His last breath and heartbeat. This is the grace of God that stirs our hearts and creates new desires within us. Do you see how Jesus went under the curse of sin and death to love you and lift you up? He went to the cross not only to save you with His blood but to sanctify, wash and cleanse you through His death and powerful resurrection!

> *"Tell me, you who want to be under the law, are you not aware of what the law says? ²² For it is written that Abraham had two sons, one by the slave woman and the other by the free woman. ²³ His son by the slave woman was born according to the flesh, but his son by the free woman was born as the result of a divine promise." Galatians 4:21-23 NIV*

Question 5: According to Galatians 4:22, what was the difference between Abraham's two sons?

_____

_____

_____

_____

Question 6: Please fill in the blanks. "His son by the slave woman was born according to the _____, but his son by the free woman was born as the result of a _____ _____" Galatians 4:23 NIV

Friends, those who are under the law are related to the "slave woman" according to "the flesh," but those who are under God's grace are related to the "free woman" through a "divine promise" and the New Covenant instituted by the blood of Christ.

> *"For this reason Christ is the mediator of a new covenant, that those who are called may receive the promised eternal inheritance—*

now that he has died as a ransom to set them free from the sins committed under the first covenant." Hebrews 9:15 NIV

Those who are in Christ are free, indeed! Free from the burden of law-keeping, free from the burden of self-efforts and achievements because Jesus set the New Covenant of grace in motion with His own death. With His own life and blood, He "ransomed" us and "set us free" from sins' burden, which drove us under its weight and power.

God's providence, sovereignty, provision, and power are all found in the death Jesus died at "just the right time" (Romans 5:6), as He hung like a criminal, exposed to the elements, and in public humiliation. What a Savior and King we serve! The grace of God wrapped up in frail humanity has appeared!

> *"For the grace of God has appeared that offers salvation to all people. [12] It teaches us to say "No" to ungodliness and worldly passions, and to live self-controlled, upright and godly lives in this present age" Titus 2:11-12*

We are either under God's law where sins mastery reigns or we are under the cross, under God's grace, where sin shall no longer be YOUR MASTER. The cross is where we find the grace of God that teaches us to say "no to ungodliness" and "worldly passions" in this present age. In other words, the cross is grace for today, tomorrow, and forever!

Question 7: Are you under God's Grace or the weight and burden of the law? Please consider your life and give an honest assessment.

SETTING CAPTIVES FREE

From A Wasteland To Bearing Fruit

*W*elcome back to the course!

Before the cross of Christ cut and healed our hearts, they were hard as stone and sick (Ezekiel 36:26; Jeremiah 17:9). We trusted in ourselves or the solutions of the world to help us get through the day, maybe not even realizing that it was our hearts that needed to be changed.

However, when we were wounded, healed, and transformed by hearing the message of the cross, we received forgiveness for our sins and healing of our hearts through Jesus' death and powerful resurrection. We entered into Jesus' death, entered into His rest, entered into His resurrection, and we rose with power, a new life free from the mantras and quick fixes of the world. Friend, this is why gospel freedom isn't like anything the world has to offer.

Man cannot offer true freedom through human/worldly counseling, and, as we'll see in our lesson today, temporal methods are void of power because their hope and healing are rooted in man's wisdom and knowledge. Freedom cannot come from within by making resolutions to "try harder" or "do better"! No, all methods of men, whether internal self-help or the systematic approach of others, "turn our hearts away from the Lord."

> *"This is what the Lord says: Cursed is the one who trusts in man, who draws strength from mere flesh and whose heart turns away from the Lord." Jeremiah 17:5 NIV*

Question 1: Please fill in the blanks: "This is what the Lord says: Cursed is the one who _____ _____ _____, who draws strength from mere flesh and whose heart _____ _____ _____ _____ _____." Jeremiah 17:5 NIV

When we trust in man, we are drawing from the knowledge and wisdom of men—drawing from man's knowledge and experience rather than the Lord's strength and power! Following man's ways, we might seem to be drawing closer to freedom, or we might think that we've entered into the "recovery" process, but the reality is, we are distracting and distancing ourselves from the lasting freedom that only Jesus can give.

Oh, friend, the love of God found at the cross draws all people to Christ (John 12:32), where our hearts are pierced, cut, removed, and replaced (Ezekiel 36:26), and where we are crucified and raised to new life (Galatians 2:20). So, it shouldn't surprise us that man's ways *"turn our hearts away from the Lord."*

> *"For my thoughts are not your thoughts, neither are your ways my ways," declares the Lord. ⁹ "As the heavens are higher than the earth, so are my ways higher than your ways and my thoughts than your thoughts." Isaiah 55:8-9*

> **Question 2:** What is the point that Isaiah 55:8-9 makes? Please expand on the thought this passage is teaching and write your thoughts here:

God's thoughts and ways are higher than man's. Higher than the heavens are above the earth. So the distance from heaven to earth is the illustration of how much higher God's thoughts and ways are to man's. Now notice the description of the person who "trusts in man," who "draws strength" from "mere flesh."

> *"That person will be like a bush in the wastelands; they will not see prosperity when it comes. They will dwell in the parched places of the desert, in a salt land where no one lives." Jeremiah 17:6 NIV*

1. Like a bush in the wastelands
2. They will not see prosperity
3. They will dwell in parched lands
4. In a salt land where no one lives

Friend, this was my life before experiencing life in Jesus' death and resurrection. I was spiritually thirsty, out in the wastelands, in a parched place in the desert and in salt lands where no one lives, and nothing grows. This description thoroughly illustrates our lives apart from Christ - desperate, isolated, wandering in the wilderness, and in urgent need for Someone powerful and strong enough to rescue us out of it.

And this is what Jesus rescued us from when He died and rose again. Jesus hung on the cross in our wastelands, parched, thirsty, and alone. He became sin under the wrath of God and was like the "bush in the wastelands" with no root, which dries up quickly, becomes a tumbleweed, and is blown away by the hot desert wind, dead!

Turning to the wisdom of man is foolish because it turns our hearts away from the Lord, and keeps us in captivity (Colossians 2:8) to sin. The world's counseling methods and efforts and programs leave us thirsty, dried out, and without roots. Although "progress" may seem to have been made through temporary behavioral changes, the very heart of the person is being drawn "away from the Lord" and therefore in the opposite direction of healing and hope, forgiveness and freedom.

> *"The Lord says: "These people come near to me with their mouth and honor me with their lips, but their hearts are far from me. Their worship of me is based on merely human rules they have been taught." Isaiah 29:13*

Question 3: According to Isaiah 29:13, what happens when we come near to God only with our mouth and lips?
- ☐ Our hearts draw near to God and our worship is rooted in God's Word
- ☐ Our hearts are far from God and our worship is based on human rules
- ☐ Our hearts draw near to God and our worship is heavenly

Human methods of behavior modification that we may have been taught cause our "hearts" to be "far from me." May we come to the cross and worship not with our lips but with our hearts that have been made new through Jesus' death. The arrows of God's wrath pierced Jesus' heart, and all who saw Him mocked Him. Jesus drank the bitter cup of God's wrath for us.

> "He pierced my heart with arrows from his quiver. [14] I became the laughingstock of all my people; they mock me in song all day long. [15] He has filled me with bitter herbs and given me gall to drink."
> Lamentations 3:13-15

Oh, friend, what does this do to your heart just now? How can we take in such love? How is it that God has this kind of love for us that He would not even spare His own Son? Can you see the love of God in the death and resurrection of Christ? Jesus poured out His life as a drink offering to fill all us believers up to the brim!

> "Sing to the Lord a new song; sing to the Lord, all the earth. [2] Sing to the Lord, praise his name; proclaim his salvation day after day." Psalm 96:1-2

Now, notice the blessing and life of the one who trusts in the Lord. If those who trust in man's strength and wisdom are the ones whose hearts are drawn away from the Lord, then those who trust in the Lord should have their hearts drawn to Him.

> "But blessed is the one who trusts in the Lord, whose confidence is in him. [8] They will be like a tree planted by the water that sends out its roots by the stream. It does not fear when heat comes; its leaves are always green. It has no worries in a year of drought and never fails to bear fruit." Jeremiah 17:7-8 NIV

1. Like a tree planted by water
2. It sends out roots by the stream

3. It does fear when heat comes
4. Its leaves are always green
5. It has no worries in drought
6. It never fails to bear fruit

What a contrast! What life we have in Christ! We are transformed from a mere tumbleweed in the desert wastelands with little to no root system, blown about by the wind, to a tree planted by the water that sends out its roots. We can bear fruit even when fear, worries, or droughts come. When we are rooted and grounded at the cross of Christ, we are like a tree planted by the water whose leaves are always green and never fails to bear fruit.

> *"Remain in me, as I also remain in you. No branch can bear fruit by itself; it must remain in the vine. Neither can you bear fruit unless you remain in me." John 15:4*

Jesus hung on the cross and poured out His blood like streams of water, and the Holy Spirit flows from His death and becomes "rivers of living water" (John 7:38) to us who believe. Nowhere can we find deeper nourishment for the roots of our hearts than in Jesus' death and resurrection, as applied by the Spirit of God. At the cross, we are blessed because Jesus was cursed (Galatians 3:13). At the cross, the Living One, whose body was prepared for this very day and purpose (Psalm 40:6) was opened up like a fountain (Zechariah 13:1-2), so we could be cleansed from sin and through the Spirit receive "rivers of living water."

Oh, friend, Jesus THE ROOT (Isaiah 11:1), and our source of life and nourishment died for our sin. The TRUE VINE (John 15:1), whose leaves are always green and never wither took on human form, was dried out, uprooted, and withered while hanging on the cross. But we, through looking at the cross and believing its message, are rooted, built up, strengthened in faith, and overflowing with thankfulness. Through Jesus, we have received a new heart, a new mind, new desires, and a completely new life. We've been forgiven and set free. We are no longer tumbleweeds in the wilderness, dry, thirsty, and alone; now, we are trees planted by the waters whose leaves are always green. What an abundant and joy-filled life we have in Christ!

"Trust in the Lord with all your heart and lean not on your own understanding; [6] in all your ways submit to him, and he will make your paths straight." Proverbs 3:5-6 NIV

Jesus "trusted in the Lord" with "all of His heart" even while His blood spilled out on the cross. He was not leaning unto His "own understanding" but "trusting" His Father all the way to Calvary no matter the cost. Through every trial, He leaned on the One who sent Him to accomplish His will, and never wavered in faith to His Father. In every way, Jesus was submissive to His Father, obedient unto death, even death on a cross! Jesus made our paths straight by becoming crooked with our sin on the cross and dying the death we deserved.

Jesus trusted God with all His heart and submitted to God perfectly and then on the cross, He removed our sin and clothed us with His perfection. Now He invites us to abide in Him, in His perfect life and death for us, to turn to Him for help in every struggle or situation, to trust Him and not man.

Question 4: Are you trusting in the Lord Jesus as your only hope, not leaning on your own understanding? Are you submitting your flesh in all its ways to its own death, just as Jesus died to remove your sin from you and raise you to new life?

The Greatest Treasure

"The kingdom of heaven is like treasure hidden in a field, which a man found and covered up. Then in his joy he goes and sells all that he has and buys that field." Matthew 13:44

Through the ages, many have searched for "hidden treasure," hoping to "strike it rich" and become wealthy overnight. These treasure hunters painstakingly search (in some cases, making it their life goal) in hopes of finding something of value. And, they think if they ever discovered that "pot of gold" at the end of the rainbow, they could become one of the wealthiest people in the world. These desires of the flesh are what the world seeks after and promotes.

Even some, in the church, teach that God's hand of favor is shown through His provision of health and wealth. But would we believers be truly satisfied with the riches, popularity, and fame of this world? Is it the "rich and famous" who arc truly happy and favored by God?

Friend, God has blessed His people with a Treasure far beyond anything this world has to offer. A Treasure that will make you one of the richest in the world instantly, upon believing and receiving Him - One that will fill you up, meet your every need, and completely satisfy you. And this Treasure searched for us and made us like a precious gem without blemish (Ephesians 5:27). Can you imagine this? Since when does the Treasure do the searching? Since Jesus Christ, the greatest Treasure ever known, came and lived among us, searched for and found us, and then died, and rose again for us. We who believe have been given Jesus, *"in whom are hidden all the treasures of wisdom and knowledge." Colossians 2:3 NIV*

Question 1: According to Colossians 2:3, how much treasure is there to be found in Jesus Christ?

_____

_____

_____

_____

This "hidden treasure" is found at the cross where Jesus Christ was put to death–"the treasure of heaven crucified." This treasure of wisdom and knowledge far outweighs and outlasts the wealth, wisdom, and knowledge of this world. This purchase of our very lives, by Jesus' very blood, wasn't temporary, but rather it lasts for all eternity. The purchase wasn't with money or wealth, which are coming to nothing, *"but with the precious blood of Christ, a lamb without blemish or defect." 1 Peter 1:19*

> *"For you know the grace of our Lord Jesus Christ, that though he was rich, yet for your sake he became poor, so that you by his poverty might become rich." 2 Corinthians 8:9*

Though Jesus was rich, He came in poverty, was pierced, and punished on the cross so that we might become rich (2 Corinthians 8:9). Rich in forgiveness and grace. Rich in love and mercy. Rich as we store up treasure in heaven where moth and rust do not destroy (Matthew 6:20). "For where your treasure is, there your heart will be also" (

> *"Again, the devil took him to a very high mountain and showed him all the kingdoms of the world and their splendor. ⁹ "All this I will give you," he said, "if you will bow down and worship me." Matthew 4:8-9*

"What good will it be for someone to gain the whole world, yet forfeit their soul? Or what can anyone give in exchange for their soul?" Matthew 16:26

As believers, we must see this world and all it has to offer for what it is - temporary. Colossians 3:1 guides us, *"Since, then, you have been raised with Christ, set your hearts on things above, where Christ is, seated at the right hand of God."*

For us who believe in Jesus, the cross is the key that opened up the treasure chest to reveal our most precious living Stone. Jesus was hung up in public and opened up for all to see, with nails in His hands, His feet, and a spear through His side. The cross revealed Jesus as the greatest Treasure, the greatest Gift, the greatest Love! Oh, friend, now we have this most valuable living Stone deep within us, in our hearts where Christ has made His home (2 Corinthians 4:7; John 14:23).

Jesus, instead of "being discovered," came to seek and save the lost (Luke 19:10)! He came to make us precious to God and without blemish (Philippians 2:15). On the cross, Jesus was opened up, and He displayed His love, forgiveness, cleansing flood, freedom, grace, mercy, and life with His shed blood. And we have this most valuable message of Treasure both to proclaim in the church and to give out to the world.

The Potter who formed us with His hands (Isaiah 64:8) has filled us with His own precious Son, *"a living stone rejected by men but in the sight of God chosen and precious"* (1 Peter 2:4). Believers are like fragile jars of clay, which can be easily broken or shattered, but because of the work Jesus has done on the cross, these mere clay pots hold the most powerful and prized possession. We have within us Jesus Christ who came to make His home with us and His dwelling place in us, *"we have this treasure in jars of clay, to show that the surpassing power belongs to God and not to us"* 2 Corinthians 4:7

> **Question 2.** "We have this _____ in jars of clay, to show
> the surpassing power _____ _____ _____ and not to us."

We're like the potter's vessel, which can be shattered into a million pieces (Psalm 2:9, Isaiah 30:14). We are weak and worn. We get tired and weary. We grow old and frail—but inside, we hold the most precious (living stone) treasure in jars of clay. At the cross, all who believe are filled with this treasure. We are filled with God's love, forgiveness, grace, mercy, wisdom, and knowledge. The purpose that we are weak and frail is to show the all-surpassing power of God in us. Our weakness and frailty show the glory of the treasure! Can you imagine that we being so fragile hold what is most valued and precious to God, and, at the same time, His all-surpassing power holds us together? "For it stands in Scripture: *"Behold, I am laying in Zion a stone, a cornerstone chosen and precious, and whoever believes in him will not be put to shame." 1 Peter 2:6*

"So we do not lose heart. Though our outer self is wasting away,
our inner self is being renewed day by day." 2 Corinthians 4:16

It is true, our "outer self" is wasting away but not so inwardly. We are renewed in our hearts as we look to Jesus and see that His Heart was pierced so ours could be healed. We look away from our circumstances and to the cross to receive strength and satisfaction. We could be poor while on this earth, but if we have Christ, then we are among the eternally rich and famous as we hold this treasure in jars of clay (2 Corinthians 4:7). So, we do not lose heart but we are renewed day by day as we find life, healing, and hidden treasure in Jesus.

> **Question 3:** What are your thoughts as you consider how you, a jar of clay have within you the most precious of treasures? Please share your thoughts.

_____

_____

_____

_____

As we conclude this lesson about Jesus being our Treasure, please read through the following passage:

"Now to you who believe, this stone is precious. But to those who do not believe, "The stone the builders rejected has become the cornerstone," and, "A stone that causes people to stumble and a rock that makes them fall." They stumble because they disobey the message—which is also what they were destined for. But you are

a chosen people, a royal priesthood, a holy nation, God's special possession, that you may declare the praises of him who called you out of darkness into his wonderful light." 1 Peter 2:7-9

Friend, to us who believe, Jesus is precious! A Treasure! Let us proclaim this message to each other in the church. And let us, as God's special possession, go out into the world and share with others how, through believing in Jesus' death and resurrection, Jesus can become their Treasure and they can become "God's special possession", too.

This message of Jesus' death for our sins and powerful resurrection from the dead needs to permeate the church, needs to be the message on the lips of all believers, as this very message is the power of God "for us who are being saved" (1 Corinthians 1:18). Then, let us go and proclaim the praises of Him who called us out of the darkness and into His wonderful light, for at the cross we have become "a chosen people, a royal priesthood, a holy nation." And at the cross *"we have this treasure in jars of clay, to show that the surpassing power belongs to God and not to us." 2 Corinthians 4:7*

Question 4: Jesus, the "treasure from heaven crucified" sought out and died for the church to make it precious and a special possession. How will knowing this help us in sharing the gospel with believers who seem to be poor in spirit and focused on the world's wealth to fill them?

Saved for Intimacy at The Cross

*I*n this lesson, we want to see the incredible intimacy Christ desires to have with His bride, the Church, and how this intimacy with Christ should affect our interactions with each other.

Jesus nourishes and cherishes the Church, desiring intimacy with her as a husband wants intimacy with his wife, in preparation for the day when Jesus will present the Church as His radiant and spotless Bride. To discover how Jesus does this, we look to His cross and "grasp how wide and long and high and deep is the love of Christ" (Ephesians 3:18).

> *"Husbands, love your wives, as Christ loved the church and gave himself up for her, [26] that he might sanctify her, having cleansed her by the washing of water with the word, [27] so that he might present the church to himself in splendor, without spot or wrinkle or any such thing, that she might be holy and without blemish. [28] In the same way, husbands should love their wives as their own bodies. He who loves his wife loves himself. [29] For no one ever hated his own flesh, but nourishes and cherishes it, just as Christ does the church, [30] because we are members of his body. [31] "Therefore a man shall leave his father and mother and hold fast to his wife, and the two shall become one flesh." [32] This mystery is profound, and I am saying that it refers to Christ and the church." Ephesians 5:25-32*

Typically, pastors and teachers use this text to talk about the relationship and intimacy husbands and wives have in their marital union. But our goal today is to focus on the intimacy between Christ and the church - our eternal relationship rather than the temporary one between husband and wife.

So, this is a message for all believers, whether you are single or married. We who are in Christ share this primary need for intimacy with Jesus. The more we see of this intimacy Christ has given to the church, the more we can love others. Since God is love (1 John 4:8), then He must pour into us before we can pour out to and love others (Romans 5:5).

> *"Husbands love your wives as Christ loved the church and gave Himself up for her." Here we are called to look to Jesus to understand true love. No one, in history, the heavens, or all the earth, but Jesus could have demonstrated such flawless and immense passion.*

The first thing we see is that Jesus "gave" Himself. Jesus Christ is a giver; He gave His life for you and me. Jesus "loved" us so much that He left His perfect and glorious home in heaven and stepped down into time and space, both of which He created and controls. But He submitted to the plan made in eternity past, humbled, limited, and diminished Himself because of His great love for us. Isn't this astonishing? Have you accepted and meditated on this truth? Have you thanked the Lord for His incredible love for you?

Question 1: What does it mean to you that Jesus "gave Himself up," that He laid down His life on the cross out of love for the Church? Please share your thoughts.

Jesus loved the church so much that He gave Himself up for her that He might sanctify her. Jesus hung on the cross, naked, covered in sin and shame; He bore the anguish of Calvary from the top of His head to the soles of His feet to save and sanctify His Bride.

Clothed in the righteousness of Christ and covered by His sacrifice, God sees us believers as spotless and without blemish. Through His death and resurrection, Jesus has set us apart for all time as uniquely His. God regards us as holy, sacred, set apart, consecrated, and dedicated to Christ.

The sacrificial and sanctifying love of Jesus is so glorious, friend, that once we experience it, we will be forever changed!

First, the love of Jesus transforms how we see ourselves! We no longer find our identity in our past or current sin struggles, but in Christ, His death and resurrection that purchased our new identity as His Bride. Jesus has washed us with the water of His Word and made us clean from our sins; so, we must no longer focus on our sin but on Jesus, our Beloved Bridegroom, who says, "You are already clean because of the word I have spoken to you." John 15:3

Second, the love of Christ for us transforms the way we view others. Are you looking at your brothers and sisters in Christ and seeing them as Christ sees them, without spot or wrinkle or any such blemish? Jesus has removed the iniquity of us all (Isaiah 53:6) so we must interact with each other not according to the flesh but according to who we are in Christ. *"From now on, therefore, we regard no one according to the flesh. Even though we once regarded Christ according to the flesh, we regard him thus no longer. Therefore, if anyone is in Christ, he is a new creation. The old has passed away; behold, the new has come." 2 Corinthians 5:16-17*

Third, the sacrificial love of Jesus transforms the way we think. *"Let each of you look not only to his own interests but also to the interests of others. Have this mind among yourselves, which is yours in Christ Jesus, who, though he was in the form of God, did not count equality with God a thing to be grasped, but emptied himself, by taking the form of a servant, being born in the likeness of men. [8] And being found in human form, he humbled himself by becoming obedient to the point of death, even death on a cross." Philippians 2:4-8*

We should have the same mind, the same focus as Jesus. We should have the same love and humility. What Jesus did on the cross was for us, and the Spirit is continuing the work in us. Does God want us to point out the faults of others or point to the One who took the blame for us all? We must look to Christ, friend, in every circumstance and situation so that we can have His mind and live a life worthy of His gospel.

As we look to Jesus and His cross, we are slowly being transformed into the image of Jesus. And if He is transforming us into His image, how are we to view our brothers and sisters in Christ? We are to see them just as we are - covered in the righteousness of Christ, and in the process of transformation. We are to view them with the eyes of faith, confident that the work Christ began in them will continue (Philippians 1:6). If we cannot get this right, how can we call unbelievers to look to the cross and be healed, loved, forgiven, and set free?

> **Question 2:** How does experiencing the sacrificial love of Jesus change the way you think and the way you view yourself and others?

Jesus gave Himself up to death on a cross to present us, His Bride, the Church to Himself in splendor, meaning glory, elevated status, in a state of high honor. Does it sound like Jesus loves His bride? Yes! He gave His own blood to make us, His Bride, *"without spot or wrinkle or any such thing, that she might be holy and without blemish."* Are you getting the idea of how Jesus Christ loves you and has loved you since before the beginning of time? I pray that you are (Ephesians 3:18)!

> *"In the same way, husbands should love their wives as their own bodies. He who loves his wife loves himself. ²⁹ For no one ever hated his own flesh, but nourishes and cherishes it, just as Christ does the church because we are members of his body." Ephesians 5:28-30*

By nature, we all love ourselves; we clothe, feed, and care for ourselves. But God invites us into a new and supernatural kind of love that is sacrificial. Jesus invites us to experience His love and then live differently.

When He died on the cross, Jesus gave up His comfort, His glory, His rights to nourish and care for His Bride. And now, ongoingly every day, Jesus nourishes us with His own body that was broken and His blood that was shed for us. He is our daily bread (John 6:54-59). Every day Jesus cherishes us by interceding for us and preparing a place for us (Hebrews 7:25, John 14:3).

Friend, Jesus was marred beyond recognition to make us His beautiful, spotless Bride (Isaiah 53:14). Willingly and with joy in His heart, He paid the price for us with His precious blood (1 Corinthians 6:20). We are now members of His body (Ephesians 5:30) united forever in His love, inseparable, and as such, we should love and care for each other.

> *"Therefore a man shall leave his father and mother and hold fast to his wife, and the two shall become one flesh. ³² This mystery is profound, and I am saying that it refers to Christ and the church"*
> Ephesians 5:31-32

Question 3: The intimacy Christ desires to have with you is comparable to the sexual intimacy between a husband and his wife.
- ☐ True
- ☐ False

The intimacy of Christ with His church is a profound mystery that was previously hidden but is now revealed. The oneness that a husband and wife experience in sexual intimacy is like the connection that Christ has with us as His Bride. Only our spiritual intimacy with Christ is far more profound, sweet, and life-giving than the physical relationship between husband and wife because our relationship with Christ is eternal and all-consuming. And this intimacy with Jesus is experienced by each believer individually and by all believers corporately.

Since we share this deep intimacy with Christ, all believers are also intimately connected. So, if we hurt one of our brothers or sisters in Christ, we are wounding the whole body of Christ. If we sin against one of our brothers or sisters, we are sinning against the entire body of Christ. Our intimacy with Christ should cause us to be all the more careful with each other. Just as Jesus, our Eternal Husband, loves and cherishes us, His body, so we should treat each other with love and respect as members of the same body.

> *"But he who is joined to the Lord becomes one spirit with him." 1 Corinthians 6: 17*

Oh, friend, look to the cross and by faith be joined with Christ as His Bride! Become one with Him in Spirit and watch your life soar into heaven as you experience the freedom, forgiveness of sins, and intense love extended to you through Jesus' death and resurrection. And as you experience the deep, intimate, nourishing love of Jesus, remember to treat your brothers and sisters in the Lord with the love and respect due to the body of Christ.

> *"So then, as we have opportunity, let us do good to everyone, and especially to those who are of the household of faith." Galatians 6:10*

Question 4: Jesus Christ loved the church so much that He gave Himself up for her. How does this affect the way you preach or teach (if you are a pastor/elder) or the way you worship in church as part of the body of Christ? Please share.

_____

_____

_____

_____

The Church's Message for Healing

*I*n Luke 5:30-32, we read, *"And the Pharisees and their scribes grumbled at his disciples, saying, "Why do you eat and drink with tax collectors and sinners?" And Jesus answered them, "Those who are well have no need of a physician, but those who are sick. I have not come to call the righteous but sinners to repentance."*

Friend, the Church is a hospital for the sin-sick. We, believers, are the "first responders," and when the sick come to us for help, we must be ready with the message of healing - the gospel.

Today, we're going to look at a passage that shows the hope, forgiveness, and freedom available through Christ for those paralyzed and trapped in sin.

We, in the Church, need to know the power of the cross for ourselves and others. We minister the gospel not only to those lost in sin but also to believers caught in sin traps. By the end of this lesson, I hope you see that it doesn't matter what the sin is or how long someone has been lost or trapped in it; what matters is that we bring the sick to Christ and His cross for healing.

> *"Now there is in Jerusalem near the Sheep Gate a pool, which in Aramaic is called Bethesda and which is surrounded by five covered colonnades. [3] Here a great number of disabled people used to lie-the blind, the lame, the paralyzed. [4] From time to time an angel of the Lord would come down and stir up the waters. The first one into the pool after each such disturbance would be cured of whatever disease he had. [5] One who was there had been an invalid for thirty-eight years. [6] When Jesus saw him lying there and learned that he had been in this condition for a long time, he asked him, "Do you want to get well?" [7] "Sir," the invalid replies, "I have no one to help me into the pool when the water is stirred.*

While I am trying to get in, someone else goes down ahead of me"
John 5: 2-7 NIV

Notice first that for thirty-eight years, this man was waiting for healing at the pool of Bethesda. Thirty-eight years is a long time. But when questioned by Jesus, "Do you want to get well?"; this man with paralysis gives a telling answer.

Jesus didn't ask a difficult question; "Do you want to get well?" The obvious answer would be, "YES! I want to get well! Please heal me!" Instead, the sick man's answer revealed that he believed it was impossible to be healed from his condition unless he could receive the help of others, "*I have no one to help me into the pool when the water is stirred. While I am trying to get in, someone else goes down ahead of me.*" (Verse 7)

> **Question 1:** Have you ever believed that some sin struggles (in your life or the life of someone else) are too long-standing or too difficult to be helped by the gospel? Please share your thoughts here.
>
> _____
>
> _____
>
> _____
>
> _____

This man had his eyes set on the healing properties of the pool, knowing he could never get there alone. And after thirty-eight years of waiting for help, it seems he had resigned himself to paralysis because even when Jesus appeared before the man asking if he wanted to experience healing, the man still kept his focus on the waters. How many people through the years have remained lost or locked up in sin because they went to the church for help only to be ignored, or worse, labeled as "addicts" and sent away to "professionals"? How many have been sitting at the pool of the church, but have not heard the message of healing, the death of Jesus for sins, and the resurrection of Jesus for justification? This should not be! As the body of Christ, we have the most powerful message in the world, and we should be proclaiming it so as to minister healing in Jesus' name (Ephesians 6:10, 2 Timothy 1:7).

Or perhaps you, yourself, are like this paralyzed man, in need of help because habitual sin (bitterness, anger, lust, gluttony, etc.) has you paralyzed. You are sin-sick, and your relationship with God, your spouse, family, and brothers and sisters in Christ are all stalled. In all areas of life, we are paralyzed by sin if we are controlled by it. Are you like the paralyzed man and blaming others? "While I am trying to get in, someone else goes down ahead of me." (John 5:7) If this is you, hear the words of Jesus to you today:

> *"Then Jesus said to him, "Get up! Pick up your mat and walk." At once the man was cured; he picked up his mat and walked. The day on which this took place was the Sabbath" John 5:8-9*

Friend, look at the love and grace of God on the cross for you. To heal you and release you from the paralysis of sin, Jesus hung on the cross without anyone to help Him, nailed solidly to the tree, paralyzed by the weight of sin, anchored to the cross to pay your penalty of sin, and free you from the power of sin!

Look up today and see Him there on the cross bleeding out a pool of healing blood to wash you in its cleansing power! See it washing over you and healing you from your sin sickness, bringing you eternal forgiveness, freedom, and cleansing. See Jesus hanging as your sin, in broad daylight, publicly displayed in humiliation, bearing your guilt and shame to purchase forgiveness and freedom for you from all your secret sins. Come today and take refuge under the cross, under the blood where we are safe, saved, sanctified, unashamed, and healed by His wounds (1 Peter 2:24).

> **Question 2:** Have you come to Jesus' healing pool of blood poured out for you at the foot of the cross? Have you washed in it and been set free by it? Please share

Look to Christ's cross and see that "at once," you are finally healed from sin's sickness: "At once the man was cured." At the cross, you were not "gradually" cured of sin and gradually forgiven; no, immediately upon belief, upon believing the message of power and love, you are healed! Our life as believers is one of ever-increasing light as we live out the gift of salvation for the rest of our lives, being sanctified steadily throughout our lives, but we are healed immediately from sin's power and sin's curse. Freedom from our slavery to sin and forgiveness is found at the cross where Jesus said to you personally, Get up! Pick up your mat and walk."

It's also exciting to see that Jesus always meets us right where we are just as He did with this man with paralysis. Jesus met this man at the pool of Bethesda, which means "house of mercy" or "the flowing water." And still, today, Jesus meets us as His house of mercy - the cross- the place where rivers of living water flow out to all who believe.

Many who come to the church will be like the paralytic man who only hoped for healing from his paralyzed state, but Jesus came to heal him (and all His people) from the inside out, making the healing full and complete! Let us experience this healing ourselves and then be ready to help others to experience it as well.

Question 3: Can you see how the gospel brings healing to those who are sin-sick? Please share.

It is important to acknowledge that there will be times when we encounter difficulties in life that cause us to doubt. We might go through hardships personally or someone might come to the church for help whose situation is extreme and appears too far gone. What do we do with doubt?

"When the men came to Jesus, they said, "John the Baptist sent us to you to ask, 'Are you the one who is to come, or should we expect someone else?'" ²¹ At that very time, Jesus cured many who had diseases, sicknesses, and evil spirits, and gave sight to many who were blind. ²² So he replied to the messengers, "Go back and report to John what you have seen and heard: The blind receive sight, the lame walk, those who have leprosy are cleansed, the deaf hear, the dead are raised, and the good news is proclaimed to the poor." Luke 7:20-22

In prison, facing death by beheading for his ministry work, John the Baptist experienced doubts about Jesus, and so, in his fear and uncertainty, he sent questions to Jesus. And Jesus quickly responded with the "good news" that the One who was to come has arrived! Jesus reassured John with the truth. From the Scriptures, John was reassured that Jesus is the long-expected Messiah. And this is the answer to our doubts today too. We look to the cross, to see that it is powerful for salvation and sanctification. Jesus is indeed the One who sets captives free, heals the sin-sick, and gives new life.

Jesus fulfilled what was spoken by the prophet Isaiah on the cross when He "took up" our infirmities and bore our diseases on it. Jesus became sin for us (2 Corinthians 5:21) that He might destroy our old man and make us new. *"For the perishable must clothe itself with the imperishable, and the mortal with immortality"* (1 Corinthians 15:53). All sin and sickness have died with Christ, and the new life has risen with Christ!

"At once the man was cured; he picked up his mat and walked. The day on which this took place was the Sabbath, ¹⁰and so the Jews said to the man who had been healed, "It is the Sabbath; the law forbids you to carry your mat," ¹¹ But he replied, "The man who made me well said to me, 'Pick up your mat and walk.' ¹²So they asked him, "Who is this fellow who told you to pick it up and walk?" ¹³The man who was healed had no idea who it was, for Jesus had slipped away into the crowd that was there" John 5:9-13 NIV

As we close out our study today, take note that this healing Jesus did was on the Sabbath, the day of rest, and this brought criticism from the religious leaders of the day.

Friend, when we anchor our testimonies to the cross of Christ and proclaim that we've been set free from years of paralyzed sinful living and then seek to help others to freedom through the gospel, we may experience criticism. There will always be "religious leaders" that want to impose rules or limits on who, when, and how people should be helped. But Jesus, the "Lord of the Sabbath," our "daily bread," and "Great Physician" is the One in whom we find our life, death to sin and self, as well as our rest and healing. We must not allow those who lack faith in Jesus to discourage or dissuade us from our gospel ministry.

Another form of discouragement can be when those we help with the gospel turn back to a life of unbelief and sin. This was the case with the man that Jesus healed, but observe how Jesus finds the man, reminds him of what God has done, and calls him to repentance.

> *"Later Jesus found him at the temple and said to him, "See, you are well again. Stop sinning or something worse may happen to you." The man went away and told the Jewish leaders that it was Jesus who had made him well." John 5:14-15*

Stop sinning, or something worse may happen to you? What could be worse than living a life of paralysis? A life in constant need of others' help? Death! Death in sin is worse, and that's where sin takes all who continue in it.

But we can come and invite others to come with us to the cross of Jesus to experience freedom from sin and its wages of death and enjoy new and abundant life through the Spirit, who teaches us to say no to ungodliness (Romans 8:2, Titus 2:12)!

Peter spoke to those who are faltering in their faith and failing to thrive spiritually when he wrote, *"For whoever lacks these qualities is so nearsighted that he is blind, having forgotten that he was cleansed from his former sins." 2 Peter 1:9*

When we see those we've helped with the gospel returning to a life of unbelief and sin, we want to remind them of what God has done for them through Jesus' death and resurrection. We want to invite them to turn from their sin and come and receive fresh cleansing at the cross.

Jesus is the only one who can heal from the paralysis of sin, breaking the chains of habitual sin and keeping all who are His from death in sin. We must come again and again to the healing waters at the foot of the cross where Jesus' blood pooled, and we were made well and healed. We come, and bring with us all who need help, to the cross and die to our old paralyzed life and rise to live our new life in Jesus. Stabilized by the gospel, we are free to carry our mat. We've died to sin and have been freed from its power over us because *"one who has died has been set free from sin" (Romans 6:7).*

Worldly counselors, teachers, and programs can only help with physical, behavioral, or outward conditions, but Jesus can heal both the physical and spiritual sin sickness of the heart. Jesus heals both our physical condition–a paralyzed life due to sin and our spiritual condition–a sin-sick heart that needs forgiveness. Only Jesus can say, "Get up! Pick up your mat and walk."

In the church, we will encounter many sin-sick people, but God has given us the message of healing for those who are lost in sin or trapped in sin: the life-giving and restorative message of the dying Lamb who atoned for our sins, the risen Lion who overcame death. The gospel of Jesus' death and resurrection to set captives free is the message that is to be proclaimed from pulpits, taught in Sunday School, interacted around in small groups. The church has one message to proclaim, both to believers and non-Christians.

"When they hurled their insults at him, he did not retaliate; when he suffered, he made no threats. Instead, he entrusted himself to him who judges justly. [24] *"He himself bore our sins" in his body on the cross, so that we might die to sins and live for righteousness; "by his wounds, you have been healed." 1 Peter 2:24-25*

Question 4: Are you seeing your role in the Church hospital for the sin-sick is to apply the medicine of the gospel to everyone at all times - in every sermon, teaching, prayer, and counseling session? Please share.

The Cross, the Shepherd, and the Flock

*D*ear friend, welcome back. You are nearing the end of this course; I hope it has been a blessing and a joy to focus on the Word of the Lord - Jesus and His gospel for the church - which endures forever (1 Peter 1:25).

In this lesson, we will consider the plea of Peter, as he was bringing his first letter to a close, appealing to the elders of the church as a fellow elder and witness.

> *"To the elders among you, I appeal as a fellow elder and a witness of Christ's sufferings who also will share in the glory to be revealed: ² Be shepherds of God's flock that is under your care, watching over them—not because you must, but because you are willing, as God wants you to be; not pursuing dishonest gain, but eager to serve; ³ not lording it over those entrusted to you, but being examples to the flock. ⁴ And when the Chief Shepherd appears, you will receive the crown of glory that will never fade away. 1 Peter 5:1-4 (NIV)*

Question 1: Please fill in the blanks. "To the elders among you, I appeal as a fellow elder and a _____ of _____ _____ who also will share in the glory to be revealed" 1 Peter 5:1

In his closing appeal to his "fellow elders," one of the first things Peter mentions is that he is not only a fellow elder but also a witness of "Christ's sufferings." Peter's heart is pleading to his fellow witnesses to remember what they saw with their own eyes - the cross and the sufferings of Christ.

Friend, as ministers of the New Covenant (2 Corinthians 3:6), we must first remember the sufferings of Christ, about which Peter and many others testify to us in the Scriptures. For if we forget the sufferings of Christ, we become void of the power of God ourselves, and go on to train up generations of biblical teachers and preachers void of the power of God, void of that which is of "first importance," and void of that power that can transform the lives of those God has put under your care. *"For when I preach the gospel, I cannot boast, since I am compelled to preach. Woe to me if I do not preach the gospel!" 1 Corinthians 9:16 NIV*

As believers in Jesus, elders, leaders, and teachers, we have been given a high calling to:

> *"Be shepherds of God's flock that is under your care, watching over them—not because you must, but because you are willing, as God wants you to be; not pursuing dishonest gain, but eager to serve" 1 Peter 5:2*

In light of the sufferings of Christ, we are to be shepherds of God's flock. If you are a pastor, teacher, leader of any kind, God has placed you in your position to care for and watch over His people. Elders have a special calling to oversee the body of Christ, but all believers are ministers of the gospel, so there is an application here for everyone.

Question 2: According to 1 Peter 5:2, what is to be our attitude as we watch over and serve the flock?
- ☐ We are to have an attitude of being above the sheep as we watch "over" them.
- ☐ We are to be willing and eager to serve.
- ☐ We are to be pursuing gain, but not dishonestly.

The undershepherd is to serve the flock with eagerness and willingness so that the congregation will sense their delight and joy in ministering the gospel to them. Others should see that we love our gospel work and that we are eager to do it. But how can we get this attitude of delight in our duties? We get it by looking long at the cross, and seeing that Jesus was willing to take our place on the cross, willing to suffer the loss of all things, willing and eager to give His life as a guilt offering for our sin. Yes, Jesus was willing and eager to die for us! *"No one takes it from me, but I lay it down of my own accord. I have authority to lay it down and authority to take it up again. This command I received from my Father" (John 10:18).*

Serving in gospel ministry is a gift! God calls us not merely to a ministry of duty, but one of great delight, giving out the message of power, love, and freedom! As we remember all that Christ has done for us, we are eager to serve others so that they, too, can experience the freedom and abundant joy-filled life Christ gives.

Christ has forgiven and set you free, transformed your heart and mind, and given you His Spirit. He has taken your past and crushed it to death on the cross. You died with Christ and have been risen with Him as a new creation. Jesus daily nourishes and cherishes you with His body broken for you and His blood shed for you. It is His sacrificial love that compels you and makes you eager to serve His people (John 6:35, 2 Corinthians 5:14, Philippians 2:13, Ephesians 2:10).

> *"not lording it over those entrusted to you, but being examples to the flock." 1 Peter 5:3.*

Question 3: What character trait does 1 Peter 5:3 teach?
☐ We are to be honest teachers.
☐ We are to be humble examples.
☐ We are to be hopeful helpers.

Gospel leaders and teachers are to be humble examples rather than "lording it over" those entrusted to our care. We have the mind of Christ (1 Corinthians 2:16), and we are to let His mind guide us in humble service as servant leaders.

Peter is repeating here the lesson he heard from Jesus. *"Jesus called them together and said, "You know that those who are regarded as rulers of the Gentiles lord it over them, and their high officials exercise authority over them. Not so with you. Instead, whoever wants to become great among you must be your servant, and whoever wants to be first must be slave of all. For even the Son of Man did not come to be served, but to serve, and to give his life as a ransom for many." Mark 10:42-45*

Jesus is Lord, but He humbled Himself to take on his favorite title, "Son of Man." And the Son of Man humbled Himself, lowering Himself down as far as He could go, serving and ransoming us as both our Shepherd and sacrificial Lamb. We who are forgiven through His sacrifice, are to follow our Good Shepherd in this trait of humility, which we get by focusing continually on the cross.

We are to "*Have this mind among yourselves, which is yours in Christ Jesus, who, though he was in the form of God, did not count equality with God a thing to be grasped, but emptied himself, by taking the form of a servant, being born in the likeness of men. And being found in human form, he humbled himself by becoming obedient to the point of death, even death on a cross.*" (Philippians 2: 5-8). Jesus humbled Himself for us, and this should be the aim of all who have died and been raised to a new life in Christ, to live in the humility of Jesus. "*To this, you were called, because Christ suffered for you, leaving you an example, that you should follow in his steps.*" 1 Peter 2:21

In all these things, we are following our Chief Shepherd who loves us and leads us in His way of gospel love!

"*And when the Chief Shepherd appears, you will receive the crown of glory that will never fade away.*" 1 Peter 5:4

Question 4: If we serve eagerly, willingly, humbly, and lovingly, look at the cross and minister the gospel to others, what do we receive from the Chief Shepherd according to 1 Peter 5:4?

_____

_____

_____

Oh, friend, a glorious day is coming when our Chief Shepherd will appear, and a crown of glory that never fades will be given to those who humbly serve others with the gospel. We look back to Christ's death and also forward to His return when we share in His glory so that we do not grow weary in our service. We remember Jesus receiving the crown of thorns that we might receive the crown of glory. We give thanks that Jesus wore our shame that we might wear and share in His glory.

Through it all, our goal is to preach Christ and Him crucified, buried, and raised from the dead to forgive sins and set captives free. In continually focusing on the humility of Jesus, who sank to death and back, and on the love of Jesus that moved Him to die for us while we were still His enemies, and on His suffering at Calvary, we learn how to minister to the sheep God has entrusted to us.

As we noted at the beginning of this lesson, "the word of the Lord remains forever." And this word is the good news that was preached to you" (1 Peter 1:25). We have received the good news of the gospel; now, we must live, preach, teach, and counsel with the powerful message of the cross. The gospel must be our theme in every sermon, every teaching, every counseling session. For this gospel is the power of God (Romans 1:16; 1 Corinthians 1:18) both for the world and the Church.

This gospel must not be assumed, hinted at, suggested, or inferred; rather, it must be proclaimed boldly, articulated clearly, and repeated often. The gospel is the reason the Scripture says:

> *"Jews demand signs and Greeks look for wisdom, [23]but we preach Christ crucified: a stumbling block to Jews and foolishness to Gentiles, [24] but to those whom God has called, both Jews and Greeks, Christ the power of God and the wisdom of God." 1 Corinthians 1:22-24*

Question 5: Please summarize the teaching of this lesson, and share what you, personally, got out of it:

_____

_____

_____

_____

The Message of Power and Wisdom for the Church

Throughout this course, we have focused on the gospel message as being not only that which brings people into the Church but also the message which sanctifies, heals, feeds, cleanses, and compels her. The gospel of Jesus Christ is the primary message that God has for His church. Everything we teach must be tethered too and flow out of this main message of Christ's death and resurrection.

Previously we looked at 1 Corinthians 1:22-24, and today we will complete our study of that passage. Here it is again:

> *"Jews demand signs and Greeks look for wisdom,* ^{23} *but we preach Christ crucified: a stumbling block to Jews and foolishness to Gentiles,* ^{24} *but to those whom God has called, both Jews and Greeks, Christ the power of God and the wisdom of God." 1 Corinthians 1:22-24*

Question 1: According to 1 Corinthians 1:22-24, "preaching Christ crucified" is...
- ☐ The power of God and the wisdom of God
- ☐ The power of man and the wisdom of God
- ☐ The power of God and the wisdom of man

Preaching Christ crucified is the power and wisdom of God! What more do we need? We need not have advanced degrees or eloquent speech to minister the gospel because we don't preach ourselves. We preach Christ - His eternal, perfect finished work on Calvary and His victorious resurrection.

And it is Christ who has qualified and equipped us (2 Corinthians 3:6, 2 Timothy 3:15-17, Hebrews 13:20-21) for the ministry!

Christ is our righteousness, giving us right standing with God. He has cleansed us from all sin, redeemed us, and set us free from captivity to sin (1 Corinthians 1:30). To experience personal transformation and also help others experience it, we must keep *"the word of the cross"* as the foundation of our faith and ministry (1 Corinthians 1:18). The word of the gospel is given in every book of the Bible, and therefore, it must be in every message we offer, and all ministry we do.

This powerful message of the cross was the "power of God" proclaimed through the preaching of the ordinary man Peter (Acts 4:13), and that message cut the hearts of those who heard it (Acts 2:37). The gospel message is what turned the "foolish Galatians" back from living in the flesh (Galatians 3:1). The gospel message turned the Thessalonians "to God and from idols" (1 Thessalonians 1:5-9). And it is the gospel message that delivers us from the kingdom of darkness, transferring us into the Kingdom of the Son He loves (Colossians 1:13). The message of Christ's death and resurrection is what saves and sanctifies the believer, so this is what we must proclaim. *"For the word of the cross is folly to those who are perishing, but to us who are being saved it is the power of God." 1 Corinthians 1:18*

> **Question 2:** What is the message of the cross to those who are perishing?
> ☐ Foolishness
> ☐ Wisdom
> ☐ Life Eternal

Preaching Christ crucified is going to be foolishness to those who are living in unbelief, but it will always be life and power to us who are being saved. So, we testify about Jesus that His death and resurrection indeed does have the power to transform lives (Philippians 3:21), heal broken hearts (Psalm 147:3), and make us completely new creations (Galatians 6:15, Ephesians 5:14, Galatians 2:20).

Finally, we next want to note that the preaching of the cross is valid and real because of the resurrection of Jesus.

"And if Christ has not been raised, our preaching is useless and so is your faith. ¹⁵More than that, we are then found to be false witnesses about God, for we have testified about God that he raised Christ from the dead. But he did not raise him if in fact the dead are not raised." 1 Corinthians 15:14-15

Can you see, from verse 14, how the resurrection of Jesus gives validity to the preaching of the cross? If Christ wasn't raised, then His death on the cross was identical to the thief's death who died next to Him, merely human and natural, and we are still in our sins. But because Jesus was raised from the dead, we can understand that the cross was the primary purpose of Jesus' coming to this earth, and His death was as our Substitute that our sins might be pardoned and removed and that we might have life.

> **Question 3:** Please fill in the blanks. "More than that, we are then found to be false witnesses about God, for we have testified about God that he _____ _____ _____ _____ _____. But he did not raise him if in fact the dead are not raised." 1 Corinthians 15:15

If the dead are not raised, we would be considered "false witnesses" because, in our preaching and teaching, we are "testifying about God" that He raised Christ from the dead. Now consider the impact on the church worldwide regarding these passages. The fact that Christ has been raised from the dead means when we preach Christ and Him crucified, we are found to be "true witnesses" of the gospel, the sufferings of Christ, and His resurrection power for the church.

Friend, in our preaching, we are testifying about Christ. This great and powerful message of the cross is the life-saving message that Jesus sent the church into the world to proclaim. The gospel is the message of "first importance" and life (1 Corinthians 15:3), peace, and hope (Romans 5:1-2) that removes hearts of stone and replaces them with hearts of flesh (Ezekiel 36:26).

> *"For if the dead are not raised, then Christ has not been raised either. 17 And if Christ has not been raised, your faith is futile; you are still in your sins." 1 Corinthians 15:16-17*

Question 4: According to 1 Corinthians 15:16-17 if Christ has not been raised…
- ☐ Your faith is strong; you are forgiven for your sins.
- ☐ Your faith is weak, but you are still forgiven for your sins.
- ☐ Your faith is futile; you are still in your sins.

"But Christ has indeed been raised from the dead, the first fruits of those who have fallen asleep." 1 Corinthians 15:20

Yes! Jesus has indeed been raised from the dead! Jesus took on flesh to put our sinful flesh to death, to free us from it, and forgive us for it. In Christ, we have died to our old lives and received the Spirit of life! If you've been transformed by the message of the cross, then you are part of the body and voice of Christ, an ambassador of Christ (2 Corinthians 5:20)!

As ambassadors, we not only represent the Lord Jesus Christ, but we speak on His behalf, *"as though God were making his appeal through us."* And if we are not speaking the message of the cross, we are not fully representing God's wisdom, nor proclaiming God's power. When Jesus hung on the cross under the wrath of God, He revealed God's mystery to the world, the message which saves the lost and also matures and sanctifies all who believe.

"We do, however, speak a message of wisdom among the mature, but not the wisdom of this age or of the rulers of this age, who are coming to nothing. 1 Corinthians 2:6

Question 5: The message of the cross is wisdom for "the mature," but not the wisdom of this world.
- ☐ True
- ☐ False

"No, we declare God's wisdom, a mystery that has been hidden and that God destined for our glory before time began. None of the rulers of this age understood it, for if they had, they would not have crucified the Lord of glory." 1 Corinthians 2:7-8

It's clear that God's wisdom, God's mystery, that which was hidden in the Old Testament, is the glorious, wonderful, terrible cross of the Lord Jesus Christ. Paul knew and understood this mystery of man being made right with God through the cross, and so, Paul decided to know nothing but "Jesus Christ and Him crucified" (1 Corinthians 2:2). By focusing on and ministering in the gospel so thoroughly, Paul could say:

> *"My message and my preaching were not with wise and persuasive words, but with a demonstration of the Spirit's power so that your faith might not rest on human wisdom, but on God's power."* 1 *Corinthians 2:4-5*

Question 6: Please summarize this lesson and share your final thoughts.

_____

_____

_____

_____

Summary

We hope you've enjoyed this study, that it has been a blessing to you, and the gospel has become more dear to you.

The Gospel for the Church course was born from a desire to see the church rediscover and return to the power of the cross! Preaching and teaching from the cross should not be relegated to a "salvation message," but rather, the gospel message should be continuously offered as the message of power from God to save, sanctify, set free, and, one day, raise and glorify all who believe.

We've noted throughout this course that all believers have the privilege of sharing the gospel with believers and non-believers alike. We share it with non-believers that they would come to salvation, and with believers to help them grow and mature in sanctification.

As we share this message with others, those that hear become near and dear to our hearts - especially when they receive the "word of the cross" with joy (1 Corinthians 1:18, 1 Thessalonians 1:6).

It should be the aim of all believers that all people would see Jesus dying on the cross for them personally, taking their sin from them and removing it as far as the east is from the west (Psalm 103:12) and that they hear Christ's word of forgiveness for them so that they might believe and turn from sin and live in the joy and worship of their Savior. But how can they see, hear, and believe unless we faithfully preach, teach, and share the good news of Christ's death and resurrection for salvation and sanctification (Romans 10:14)?

Let us summarize this study by reflecting on an event that happened after the resurrection of Jesus:

> "Now Thomas, one of the twelve, called the Twin, was not with them when Jesus came. ²⁵So the other disciples told him, "We have seen the Lord." But he said to them, "Unless I see in his

hands the mark of the nails, and place my finger into the mark of the nails, and place my hand into his side, I will never believe." John 20:24-25

Question 1: According to John 20:25, what did Thomas say he needed to believe that Jesus rose from the dead?

_____

_____

_____

_____

What was it that Thomas wanted?

Oh, friend, do you hear the cry of those lost in unbelief and those to whom you preach, counsel, or sit next to in church? They want to see Jesus! God must give them spiritual eyes to look at the cross and see Jesus' being wounded for their transgressions and bruised for their iniquity. It is our role to point them to the cross and invite them to see and touch, that is, to experience the power of the cross personally.

Now, notice what happens when people actually see the cross and the wounds of Jesus for them:

> *"Eight days later His disciples were again inside the house, and Thomas was with them. Jesus came, though the doors had been barred, and stood among them and said, "Peace to you." [27] Then He said to Thomas, "Reach here with your finger, and see My hands; and put out your hand and place it in My side. Do not be unbelieving, but [stop doubting and] believe." [28] Thomas answered Him, "My Lord and my God!" John 20:26-28 (Amplified Bible - AMP)*

Can you imagine this scene? Thomas was standing right before the risen Lord, standing there touching Him. Thomas felt Jesus' pierced hands and wounded side, which proved and testified that Jesus willingly stretched Himself out on the cross, died, and rose back to life for him.

Question 2: What was Thomas' response when He saw and touched the wounds of Jesus?

_____

_____

_____

_____

Consider the scene as Thomas put his hand into the side of Jesus that poured out blood and water to cleanse and forgive him personally for every sin. Jesus invited Thomas into this intimate experience! And then we see Thomas' response of not only belief but pure worship: *"My Lord and my God!"*

Friend, we cannot invite others to see and touch Jesus physically, but we can invite them to see Jesus spiritually, and Jesus says there is a special blessing for these: Jesus said to him, *"Have you believed because you have seen me? Blessed are those who have not seen and yet have believed."* And again, we read, *"Though you have not seen him, you love him. Though you do not now see him, you believe in him and rejoice with joy that is inexpressible and filled with glory."*

Our mission is to point people to the cross, to invite them to see with the eyes of their heart the wounds of Jesus (Ephesians 1:18). As God's appointed leaders in the church, we are to bring believers continually before the cross and invite them into the ongoing personal experience of seeing by faith the One who loved them and gave Himself for them so that they may worship in spirit and truth.

And this is also our goal as we go and make disciples of all nations as well! We invite them to see the wounds in Jesus' hands and feet and the spear that was thrust into His side, the crown of thorns He wore, and the stripes on His back. We help them to see that Jesus suffered in this way to forgive their sins, and to purchase them for God, enabling them to worship with us.

> *"And they sang a new song [of glorious redemption], saying,*
> *"Worthy and deserving are You to take the scroll and to break its*
> *seals; for You were slain (sacrificed), and with Your blood, You*
> *purchased people for God from every tribe and language and*
> *people and nation" (Revelation 5:9 AMP).*

Our role as believers is to invite all people to look at the cross and see Jesus, who took up our pain and bore our sufferings (Isaiah 53:4). In this course, we have wanted you to see the living One who rose from the grave with the marks of victory in His hands, proving His love for you. We wanted you to touch the scars and marks of Jesus' finished work where He battled for your life, where He died for you and won!

Question 3: In this study, have you seen Jesus and the wounds He received for you? Please share:

_____

_____

_____

_____

Our deepest desire is to reach both the church and the world with the gospel of Jesus Christ, to see one more heart cut and healed at the cross! One more marriage restored! One more life living in freedom from slavery to sin! One more heart rejoicing in the work of the cross! One more life resurrected from the dead, one more life made alive in Christ! (Romans 6:11; Ephesians 2:1; 5)

"Now to him who is able to do immeasurably more than all we ask or imagine, according to his power that is at work within us, [21] to him be glory in the church and in Christ Jesus throughout all generations, for ever and ever! Amen." Ephesians 3:20-21

www.ingramcontent.com/pod-product-compliance
Lightning Source LLC
Chambersburg PA
CBHW081227090426
42738CB00016B/3218